"In the first place [the church] can ask the state whether its actions are legitimate and in accordance with its character as state, i.e., it can throw the state back on its responsibilities. Secondly, it can aid the victims of state action. The church has an unconditional obligation to the victims of any ordering of society, even if they do not belong to the Christian community (!). The third possibility is not just to bandage the victims under the wheel, but *to put a spoke in the wheel itself."*

— Dietrich Bonhoeffer
on the church's possible
action toward the state

Dietrich Bonhoeffer

A Spoke in the Wheel

RENATE WIND

Translated by John Bowden

WILLIAM B. EERDMANS PUBLISHING COMPANY
GRAND RAPIDS, MICHIGAN

First published 1990 as *Dem Rad in die Speichen fallen: Die Lebensgeschichte des Dietrich Bonhoeffer* by Beltz Verlag, Weinheim and Basel
© 1990 by Beltz Verlag

English translation © 1991 by John Bowden
First English edition published 1991 as *A Spoke in the Wheel: A Life of Dietrich Bonhoeffer*, by SCM Press Ltd
26-30 Tottenham Road, London N1 4BZ
This edition published 1992 by special arrangement with SCM by
Wm. B. Eerdmans Publishing Co.
255 Jefferson Ave. SE, Grand Rapids, MI 49503
Printed in the United States of America
Library of Congress Cataloging-in-Publication Data

Wind, Renate, 1950-
[Dem Rad in die Speichen fallen. English]
Dietrich Bonhoeffer : a spoke in the wheel /
Renate Wind ; translated by John Bowden.
p.   cm.
Translation of: Dem Rad in die Speichen fallen.
Includes bibliographical references.
ISBN 0-8028-0632-5
1. Bonhoeffer, Dietrich, 1906-1945. 2. Theologians — Germany — Biography.
I. Title.
BX4827.B57W55   1992
230'.044'092 — dc20
[B]   92-3653
                                                              CIP

ACKNOWLEDGMENTS

We gratefully thank the following archives, publishers, and persons for granting permission to reprint the photographs in this book.

Page 94, bottom: Pastor Otto Dudzus, Cologne. Page 150, top left: Karl Barth Archives, Basel; bottom left: Barbara Bayer, Wuppertal. Page 165, top right: Douglas R. Gilbert, Newburryport. All other photos are from the book *Dietrich Bonhoeffer: Bilder aus seinem Leben*, edited by E. Bethge, R. Bethge, and C. Gremmels (Munich: Christian Kaiser Verlag, 1986); ET *Dietrich Bonhoeffer: A Life in Pictures* (London: SCM; Minneapolis: Fortress, 1986).

CONTENTS

Chronological Table   VII

Introduction   IX

Having a Place in the World   I
1906-1914

The Dream of a Fine, Devout Death   13
1914-1918

Knowing Where One Stands   19
1919-1923

Understanding what the Church Is   25
1923-1924

Communion of Saints   32
1925-1927

"The earth remains our mother"   41
1928-1930

"Who would wish unconcernedly and
uncaringly to enter the promised land?"   48
1930-1931

"Consider what is on earth!"   56
1931-1932

A Spoke in the Wheel   65
1933

"Open your mouth for the dumb"   78
1933-1934

Ban War!   89
1934-1935

"Whoever knowingly separates himself from the
Confessing Church separates himself from salvation"   99
1935-1936

"Only those who cry out for the Jews
may sing Gregorian chant!"   113
1936-1938

"Come before winter!"   127
1939

The Masquerade of Evil   139
1940-1943

Learning to Believe in the
This-Worldliness of Life   155
1943-1944

The End Is the Beginning   172
1944-1945

Bibliography   181

CHRONOLOGICAL TABLE

1906   Dietrich Bonhoeffer born in Breslau, 4 February

1912   Family moves to Berlin

1914–18   First World War

1919   Beginning of the Weimar Republic

1923   Dietrich leaves school and begins his theological studies in Tübingen

1924   Study visit to Rome; from the summer semester, studies in Berlin

1927   Gains doctorate with *Sanctorum Communio*

1928   First theological examination; beginning of probationary ministry in Barcelona

1930   Second theological examination and qualification for university teaching with thesis *Act and Being*, in Berlin; September, beginning of study visit to Union Theological Seminary, New York

1931   Return to Berlin, as assistant lecturer and auxiliary preacher in Prenzlauer Berg; youth secretary for the World Alliance of Churches

1933   Hitler seizes power; Bonhoeffer becomes involved in building up a church opposition to the attempts of the state to "coordinate" the church; lecture on "The Church and the Jewish Question"; October, takes a pastorate in London

1934   Takes part in the ecumenical conference at Fanö; "Peace Sermon" there

1935   Return to Germany; becomes head of the Preachers' Seminary of the Confessing Church in Finkenwalde, near Stettin

1936   Study trip by the seminary to Sweden; permission to teach withdrawn

1937   Closure of the Preachers' Seminary by the Gestapo; further work in illegal collective pastorates; *The Cost of Discipleship* published

1939   Journey to America to take on a visiting lectureship in New York; return to Germany three weeks later; Second World War breaks out

1940   Beginning of involvement in conspiracy as a courier for the resistance group in the Abwehr

1941   Conversations with representatives of the ecumenical movement in Geneva; work on *Ethics*

1942   Journey to Norway; meeting with Bishop George Bell

1943   Becomes engaged to Maria von Wedemeyer; April, arrested; in the Wehrmacht prison of Tegel, Berlin; *Letters and Papers from Prison*

1944   Failure of attempt on Hitler's life; after the discovery of the "Zossen documents," Bonhoeffer is moved to the Gestapo basement in Prinz-Albrecht-Strasse

1945   February, taken to Buchenwald concentration camp; April, transported to Schönberg, then to Flossenbürg concentration camp; executed on 9 April

INTRODUCTION

THE PRISONER IN CELL 92 OF TEGEL MILITARY PRISON IN Berlin is a special case. Dietrich Bonhoeffer, aged thirty-seven, a lecturer in theology and a pastor banned from teaching, most recently acting as a courier for the Abwehr, arrested on suspicion of conspiracy against the Führer and the Reich, is the star prisoner. He comes from those better-class circles which so far have not been associated with conspiracy against the state. For years his father has been head of the Berlin clinic, the Charité, and his uncle is City Commandant of Berlin. In 1943 a man with such connections is still a rare phenomenon in the prisons of Hitler's Germany. So the prison staff is not sure how to treat him. The warders in Tegel prison have clear images of those who are their enemies. Anyone sent here is either a "Bolshevik agent," a "destroyer of morale," a "cowardly deserter," or simply a "Communist swine." So anyone in this prison may with impunity be abused as a "hooligan" and be victimized as an "enemy of the state." However, one cannot take that tone with the new occupant of cell 92. Nor does he fit into any of the usual categories. He is not where he belongs.

Sometimes he himself seems to feel the same way. The question of Dietrich Bonhoeffer's own identity often comes up in his *Letters and Papers from Prison*. In the summer of 1944, he wrote a poem "Who am I?" In it we find the portrait of someone made up of contradictions, who emerges from his cell "calmly, cheerfully, firmly, like a squire from his country house," and who at the same time, like his fellow prisoners, gets "stir-crazy," and has to fight against anxiety and depression. Under the pressure of the interrogation prison, which goes on for months, urgently waiting for the overthrow of Hitler which he has had a share in preparing — and which will then go wrong, only a few days later — Dietrich develops as a theme the way in which he is torn in two directions, between self-confidence and doubt in himself. This contradiction dogged him all his life, and it was never just a problem for him as an individual. The reason why Dietrich felt this problem so strongly was that during the course of his life traditional values were both put in question and put to the test.

Dietrich came from a family in which people knew who they were and where they stood. For him that became a question which was constantly reopened and constantly had to be given a new answer. It was not easy to give a credible answer to it, since the world which had shaped him did not remain the same.

Having a Place
in the World

―――――――― 1906–1914 ――――――――

WHEN DIETRICH BONHOEFFER WAS BORN ON 4 FEBRUARY
1906 in Breslau, the world was still in order. His childhood
years fell in a period which was later to be called "the good old
days." The beginning of the new century had been celebrated in
1889 with the World Fair in Paris. In the catalogue of the Fair,
one could read: "This international exposition is the magnificent
result, the mighty summing up, of a whole century of the richest
discoveries and the most amazing sciences. . . . This century is
coming to an end and at the same time opening up a new era in
human history." Such a solemn and optimistic statement
matched the spirit of the time. There was far more dispute over
the Eiffel Tower, which had been built shortly before the World
Fair, than over the sentiments quoted here.

Dietrich was the sixth of eight children. His father, Karl
Bonhoeffer, was professor of psychiatry and head of the clinic
in Breslau. His mother Paula was a von Hase by birth. Her
father was a professor of theology and for a time court preacher
to Kaiser Wilhelm II. The family in which Dietrich grew up
was among the cultural élite of the German Reich.

I

The Bonhoeffers lived in a spacious house with a garden. On the wall in the entrance hall, painted on canvas, hung the family tree: it could be traced back to the sixteenth century. Dietrich's father's ancestors were reputable citizens. The family of Karl Bonhoeffer was proud of its middle-class origins. They had little respect for Paula Bonhoeffer's aristocratic relatives. At a very early age Paula had dissociated herself from her milieu. Instead of preparing for a marriage in keeping with her status, she trained as a teacher and eventually married a middle-class husband, though really another man had been intended for her.

At the beginning of the twentieth century it was clear that the future belonged to the middle classes. True, the monarchy still ruled in Germany, and the aristocracy and the army were the "pillars of society," but the factories and commercial offices, the research laboratories and the professorial chairs, had long been taken over by the middle class. They guaranteed economic, scientific and technological progress. That made them self-confident.

Karl Bonhoeffer was a typical *fin de siècle* academic. He was convinced that the world could be investigated and understood. He had no time for speculation, whether religious or scientific. So he had no time either for Sigmund Freud, his fellow-psychiatrist in Vienna. He found sinister Freud's claim that human beings are far more dependent on their unconscious impulses and drives than they think. Such an attitude was against his way of thinking and living. For him, science was empirical research and a rational explanation of demonstrable phenomena. His personal program was to get to know reality and cope with it rationally. He wanted to bring up his children, daughters as well as sons, to do that too.

Dietrich was the youngest of four sons. A photograph

from 1910 shows him at four years of age with his father and three older brothers, Karl-Friedrich, Walter, and Klaus. Dietrich is an attractive small boy with long blonde hair and a pale, girlish face. He looks different from the other males in his family. His older brothers take after their father; they are youthful and slim and have a watchful, skeptical look on their faces. They share their father's scientific interests. He can do something with them.

Dietrich, the somewhat dreamy little one, did not find it easy to assert himself against his brothers. Above all he had to fight for recognition from his father, who identified far more with his older sons. Even as an adult, Dietrich wanted to be accepted by his father. That does not mean that he later brought this conflict out and engaged in it openly. Karl Bonhoeffer's authority was far too undisputed for that. But in later remarks Dietrich described the "austerity" of the father-son relationship as being both demanding and disquieting at the same time. And in periods of crisis in his life he wrote down childhood memories, self-critical reflections, which give some indications of the needs and conflicts of Dietrich Bonhoeffer the child: "Even in his boyhood he had liked imagining himself on his death-bed, surrounded by all those who loved him, speaking his last words to them. Secretly he had often thought about what he would say at that moment."[1]

Being at the center of things, for once being noticed by everyone, is the fantasy of children who find it difficult to stand up for themselves to parents and siblings.

During Dietrich's childhood his parents were preoccupied with five adolescents who were in the process of becoming

---

1. Bethge, *Bonhoeffer*, 24. Bibliographical details of this and other books cited regularly appear in the Bibliography.

grown-ups, Dietrich's brothers and his sisters Ursula and Christine. In addition they had an increasing number of social obligations. Dietrich was one of the three little ones who followed on behind. At least among them he was dominant. For his sisters Sabine and Susanne he was the hero. This family grouping explains why later Dietrich had simultaneously to fight for attention and to try not to dominate.

When Dietrich was six, the family moved to Berlin. There Karl Bonhoeffer took over the chair of psychiatry and neurology, a leading position at the time, and became Director of the famous university clinic, the Berlin Charité. He was now a privy councilor; he had access to the highest figures in the government, and was the leading representative of German psychiatry and an internationally recognized authority, with private patients from both Germany and abroad. And in all this he embodied the Prussian virtues of the German cultural élite: a sense of duty, understatement, "being more than one appears."

In this and many other respects the Bonhoeffers were typical of the life-style and sensibilities of the enlightened, conservative-liberal middle class of the time. For all the tolerance, there was a patriarchal régime in the family. Karl was an institution. Even at home he did not just belong to his family. He had a study which the children were not allowed to enter. In all family matters he had the last word. But he was bothered only with the really important problems.

That does not mean that Karl Bonhoeffer did not care for his family. On the contrary, all the children remembered him as an enthusiastic father. However, the ways in which father and children encountered one another were strictly regulated. Great importance was attached to family meals. But in Dietrich's family, too, at table children spoke only when they were spoken to. If it could be arranged, Karl would spend part of the evening in the family circle. He regularly read aloud, from the works of Schiller, Dostoievsky, and Fontane. A photograph from the family album shows him here as the undisputed center of the household, around whom the whole family gathered as a matter of course. The middle class of the Wilhelmine era loved such pictures of the family as a self-contained, well-ordered world.

The children were unanimous in describing their father as a man who was both sensitive and detached. He himself expresses in his memoirs the conviction that "the qualification to be a psychiatrist must also show itself not only in the development of an understanding for those who think differently, but also in control of the emotions to a special degree."[2]

That was not only a dig at his colleague Freud, but a criterion for judgments and decisions. With such an attitude one could reduce great words and fine feelings to their substance. Karl Bonhoeffer also did that with his children. He showed them that he would not stand any nonsense. That trained them to be matter-of-fact and honest. Sabine, Dietrich's twin sister, recalled: "His dismissal of fine words at times made us monosyllabic and uncertain, but it meant that as we grew up we no longer had a taste for slogans, gossip, commonplaces and verbosity."[3]

That was one side. On the other side, some of the children also suffered under their father's detachment. Even as a grown woman, Susanne, the youngest daughter, remembered her feelings on one of the rare visits that she paid to her father in his clinic, to take an old toy to give to the sick children. There she

---

2. Memoirs of Karl Bonhoeffer, in *Karl Bonhoeffer. Zum hundertsten Geburtstag*, Berlin, Heidelberg and New York 1969, 76f.

3. Leibholz-Bonhoeffer, *Vergangen*, 24.

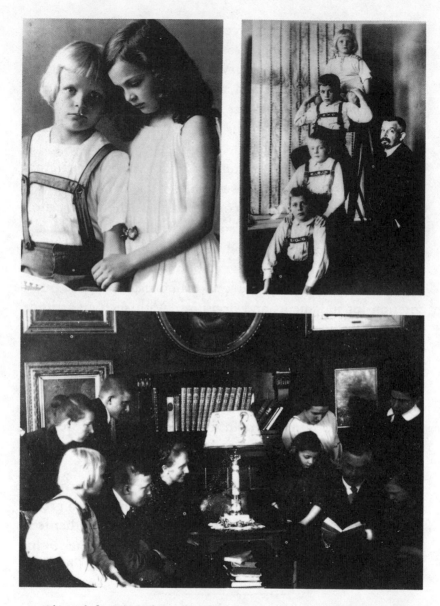

Above left: *Dietrich Bonhoeffer with his twin sister Sabine, 1914*
Above right: *Karl Bonhoeffer with his sons, 1910*
Below: *The Bonhoeffer family reading together, around 1913*

found a man who showed far more signs of affection to the sick children than to his own, and who even let them touch him: "When we parted, I felt very fond of my father and wanted to touch him and stroke him like the sick children, but I didn't dare."[4]

Letting oneself be touched, showing feelings, sharing oneself spontaneously with another person — you didn't learn any of this from such a father. But there was nothing special about that. In upper-middle class circles, keeping a distance was thought to be good form, and self-control was a virtue that was especially prized. Karl Bonhoeffer had himself been brought up to have such an attitude. He passed on with a good conscience what he took for granted, that one kept one's emotional life under control. Anything that continued to go on in the unconscious and was repressed was another matter.

Admitting feelings and being allowed to show them was a woman's business. Women were to embody the emotional element, alongside male rationality. This division of roles also applied with the Bonhoeffers. However, for Paula Bonhoeffer, to have feelings and to show them was also an expression of her sovereignty. Even as a young girl she would not be told, and as Karl Bonhoeffer's wife she also preserved her independence. She expressed her feelings so openly and naturally that this was accepted, even by her husband. At the same time she made it clear that feeling and understanding go together.

Paula Bonhoeffer taught her children herself in the first years of their schooling. She thought nothing of Prussian education. She often expressed the view that Germans had their

---

4. Quoted from the unpublished memoirs of Susanne Dress, née Bonhoeffer, which were made available to me by Professor Andreas Dress and Heidi Dress of Bielefeld.

spines broken twice in life, first at school and then in the army. The children enjoyed her teaching. It was lively, and stimulated them to thoughts and discoveries of their own. Some of her pupils later got terribly bored in school and were the terror of those teachers for whom quietness and order were the first duty of a citizen and the supreme goal of learning.

"Bonhoeffer bit the model" was put down in the class book when Klaus ate the cherries he was supposed to be painting. His parents took a relaxed view of this incident, as of many of a similar kind. Dishonesty or reluctance to help were worse. Paula Bonhoeffer, who had not forgotten her own youthful urge for freedom, gave her children a space to breathe in which was unusual for the time. For years she was responsible for the social and emotional side of their upbringing. She told stories, including stories from the Bible, and the children learned songs and poems from her. She was the source of information, responding to questions, needs, and problems at all stages of their lives.

Of the boys, Dietrich was most like her: musical, sensitive, interested in people and their stories. From his boyhood Dietrich was the one who most clearly had a feminine side, and not just in appearance. However, it was still almost inconceivable to his generation and the circles in which he lived that this should be accepted and expressed. Dietrich wanted to be a "real man" like his father and brothers. At all events, later he often related how he had changed decisively under the influence of his father. Evidently all his life he attempted to compensate for the psychological make-up which he had inherited from his mother and to control it by means of the norms taken over from his father. The sometimes exaggerated detachment which many people observed in him later may also be connected with the fact that he really was quite different.

Although both parents played an important role for Dietrich, in his childhood he had no fixation on either his father or his mother. The reason for this was that at the time middle-class families were not at all like our present small nuclear families. While the family was the undisputed point of reference and focal point, right up into adult life, it did not consist only of the closest members of the family.

The household included the cook, the chambermaid, the chauffeur, and the governess, who was usually unmarried and lived in the house "as one of the family." For Dietrich and his brothers and sisters, the family circle sometimes also included relatives who were taken in for a while: unmarried or widowed aunts, older cousins studying in Berlin, and grandmother, who joined her son's family at the age of eighty. The house was a large one and open to guests. Uncles and cousins came on visits, Karl's colleagues and students were invited, and gradually more and more friends would come from the neighborhood, including admirers, fiancés, and fiancées of the older children. Dietrich grew up in a home which was open to a great variety of encounters and influences. In such a climate, intelligent and interested children automatically took in a vast amount, sometimes even more than was good for them.

The wide range of family relatives and friends was by no means uniform in views and life-styles. In Karl's middle-class family there were conservative monarchists and liberal republicans, and among Paula's aristocratic ancestors and relatives there were some rebels, including one person who had been involved in the occupation of the Hohenasperg fortress, because in 1848 he was a supporter of the Republic.

Even at the family table, the children of Karl and Paula Bonhoeffer learned that it was possible to have different views about the monarchy and society in the Kaiser's Germany. The

9

Bonhoeffers did not share the secret admiration that a large part of the German middle class felt for the aristocracy and the Hohenzollern dynasty. They were highly amused at the sailor suit which the Kaiser's love of the fleet had popularized, and mocked the governess, who had an excessive admiration for the Prussian royal house; Karl-Friedrich taught his small sister that "in any case the aristocracy is rubbish."[5] They had only mild contempt for the tasteless pomp, the sentimental Germanic cult, and the Kaiser's Prussian maxims. But they also had little sense of the danger lurking in the wings, behind the self-congratulatory atmosphere which surrounded the monarchy. All this was regarded as a flaw in a world which was by and large in order. There was a belief that peace had been secured at home and abroad. Prosperity and progress, reason and stability seemed to be the foundation for the new century. At that time, at any rate, only a few people recognized that under the surface of the "good old days" political and social conflict was looming, and that the foundations were fragile. They had found themselves a place in society, and they would fill it responsibly.

So the world of Dietrich's childhood was a whole world. Later he would say that his home had protected him from the shadow side of life. There were no anxieties about clothing, lodging, and food; there were enough toys and books, a place for friends, a room of his own, the garden, the holiday home in the Harz mountains. But more than that distinguished the Bonhoeffer children from their contemporaries in the working-class areas. Many years later, in his prison cell in Tegel, Dietrich was to bring out the decisive difference in a fragment of a play. In it the proletarian Heinrich says to Christoph, the

---

5. Ibid.

son of a middle-class family: "You have a foundation, you have ground under your feet, you have a place in the world. . . . "[6]

That was the real advantage which Dietrich had over others: he knew where he came from and who he was. He had parents who had already become something, and a family history of which he could be proud. Traces of famous people from past and present were all around him in his home. In the Bonhoeffer household, names which others knew only from *Who's Who* or from dictionaries were in the visitors' book or the family chronicle.

Anyone who grows up like this has things easier than others. From the start he has a different awareness of himself. He is one of the élite, of those who have a share in determining what goes on in the world. Of course that also means that he has an obligation to this daily tradition. He has to be one of the best, he has to show quite special qualities. Apparently the Bonhoeffers took it just as much for granted that they could live up to these expectations as they took for granted the expectations themselves.

At any rate, Dietrich had little difficulty here. He learned quickly and well, and was both an imaginative child and a good sportsman. At seven and a half he went to the grammar school. He did well, but he was no swot and no stay-at-home. What he did outside school was in keeping with the interests of a seven-year-old: reading adventure stories and building dens, making music and playing basketball. And the first list of presents which he wrote all by himself shows what else he wanted, like all small boys: "Pistols with corks, soldiers."

War games were a popular pastime in the Kaiser's Ger-

---

6. Bonhoeffer, *True Patriotism*, 214.

many. Military parades and maneuvers, colorful and bombastic, were at the same time a demonstration of power and a popular attraction. From time to time the great European powers exchanged militaristic threats; the German Kaiser was particularly unattractive with his sabre-rattling. But it was reckoned that the military equilibrium of the highly armed European nations would insure peace, and there was a conviction that in the end of the day everyone, even the Kaiser, was for peace. Many people failed to realize that the generals wanted to try out their new weapons and that the major industries wanted a new division of markets and new sources of raw material.

When Dietrich was eight, the First World War began. The internal and external stability of the "good old days" had proved deceptive. "The lights are going out all over Europe." What had seemed to be a sound world was coming unstuck, and it would never return to its old order, not even for Karl and Paula Bonhoeffer and their family.

The Dream of a Fine,
Devout Death

———————— 1914–1918 ————————

GENERAL MOBILIZATION WAS DECLARED IN GERMANY ON
1 August 1914. There was a festival mood in the streets.
The Bonhoeffer children were infected with it. Dietrich's oldest
sister Ursula stormed into the house from the street shouting,
"Hurrah, there's a war" — and was boxed on the ears. War was
a serious matter.

The élite of German culture did not want the war, but
believed that it was inevitable. According to the official version,
attack was the best form of defense against the encirclement
of the "Axis powers," which were obstructing the "place in the
sun" in the face of the intensified competition offered by Germany; they wanted to force a war. In this situation, no one
was willing to leave the Fatherland in the lurch. Even the Social
Democrats did not want to be seen to be unpatriotic. Against
the votes of Rosa Luxemburg and Karl Liebknecht, on 4 August
they sided with the government over war credits. The Kaiser
proclaimed: "I no longer see any parties, I see only Germans."
Both Roman Catholic and Protestant pastors preached "God
with us!" Soldiers wrote graffiti on the trains to the front,

"Every shot a Russian, every thrust a Frenchman," and waved good-bye as though they were off to a shooting party.

This kind of enthusiasm over the war was far from being the attitude of the Bonhoeffers. But they were convinced of the justice of the German war aims and did their "duty for the Fatherland." War loans were taken out, and like thousands of other university professors Karl Bonhoeffer signed a declaration: "It fills us with dismay that the enemies of Germany are seeking to contrast the spirit of German learning with what they call Prussian militarism. The spirit in the German army is just the same as that in the German people. Service in the army makes our youth fit for all the works of peace, since it trains them for self-denial and a sense of duty, and gives them the self-awareness and sense of honor of the truly free man who willingly subordinates himself to the whole. It is our belief that salvation for the whole of European culture depends on the victory which the German military will achieve, on the discipline, the loyalty, and the readiness for sacrifice of a united German people."[1]

German children and young people were brought up on such sentiments. The feeling that "the world will be healed by the German spirit" was to last long after the First World War. Dietrich, too, would only gradually put in question the values on which the salvation of European culture was supposed to hang.

Day by day he and his schoolfriends marked out the latest front. In every classroom hung a map of Europe on which the advance of the German armies was documented with black, white, and red flags. But then the front came to a standstill.

---

1. Documented in *Unser Jahrhundert im Bild,* Gütersloh 1964, 192.

There were rumors of pitched battles, trench warfare, and poison gas. The wider Bonhoeffer family had its first war dead.

The death of their older cousins preoccupied Dietrich and his twin sister Sabine until late into the night: "We lay awake a long time and tried to imagine what eternal life and being dead were like. We endeavored every evening to get a little nearer to eternity by concentrating on the word 'eternity' and excluding any other thought."[2]

The two ten-year-olds were not the only ones to be preoccupied with such existential questions. The war which refused to end made the public very aware of death. The church was entrusted with the task of strengthening the will to prevail. In 1917 the *Allgemeine Lutherische Kirchenzeitung* published a quotation from an address by Reinhold Seeberg, the professor of theology who was later to supervise Dietrich's doctorate: "Fight on and endure! Bear witness everywhere to a German peace! We trust in the sound sense of our people, in our army and its leaders, in the German heart of our Kaiser, in God. German peace is the peace of victorious culture. May God give us this German peace."[3] This speech became a manifesto against any possible peace treaty on the basis of the existing frontiers. German peace meant gaining territory for Germany.

The slogans about enduring led to the romanticizing of death. Patriotic songs and postcards glorified the death of soldiers. Humanistic teachers bandied Horace's line "It is sweet and honorable to die for one's country." Bertolt Brecht, at a grammar school in Augsburg, barely escaped relegation when

---

2. Bethge, *Bonhoeffer*, 23.
3. Documented in Günter Brakelmann, *Der deutsche Protestantismus im Epochenjahr 1917*, Witten 1974, 103.

he wrote in an essay on Horace that in an emergency this court jester "would have been the first to run away."[4]

By contrast, Dietrich's feelings and thoughts seem to have inclined more towards the Fatherland and readiness for sacrifice. He enthusiastically read the stories of people who sacrificed their lives for a good cause. For the sensitive and imaginative boy these thoughts of death became a constant preoccupation. Dietrich was fascinated with the question how one might face death. In the reflections from 1932 which I have already mentioned, he describes what was going through his mind at that time: "He would have liked to die young, to die a fine, devout death. He would have liked them all to see and understand that to a believer in God dying was not hard, but was a glorious thing."[5]

But the dream of a fine, devout death had its snags. Dietrich longed for death and at the same time feared it, for he was also very fond of life. Sometimes he enjoyed his life so intensely that the family noticed it. When provisions became scarce at the end of the war, even in upper-middle class families, Dietrich developed unexpected skills in organizing food. He was very fond of eating, and of eating as well as possible.

This vital and sensual affirmation of life clashed with the longing for death. Dietrich recalled: "In the evening when he went to bed over-tired, he sometimes thought that it was going to happen. . . . Then in his innocence he cried out to God, asking to be granted a deferment. These experiences dismayed him to some extent. For obviously he did not want to die, he was a coward. . . . He was ready to die, it was only his animal

---

4. Werner Hecht, Hans-Joachim Bunge, Käthe Rülicke-Weiler, *Bertolt Brecht. Sein Leben und Werk*, Berlin 1969, 13.
5. Bethge, *Bonhoeffer*, 24.

nature that again and again made him contemptible in his own eyes, that led him away from himself."[6]

It is certainly no coincidence that Dietrich recalled this particular scene as a grown man. As with many sensitive and lively people, these inner conflicts remained with him all his life. Dietrich continually tried to reconcile the two sides; readiness for sacrifice and a bent for the good life; voluntary renunciation and the enjoyment of life; a longing for death and an affirmation of life.

However, his childhood vision of a fine, devout death vanished to the degree that real life was threatened by real death. In 1917 his older brothers were called up. They could have avoided immediate danger through their father's contacts, but they reported to the infantry, "because there the need is greatest."[7]

In April 1918 Walter Bonhoeffer was seriously wounded. He dictated a letter home three hours before his death: "Here too I have to keep up my technique of not thinking about pain. However, there are more interesting things in the world than my wound. Mount Kemmel and its possible consequences and the news that we have now occupied Ypres give us a good deal of hope. . . ."[8]

These lines sum up the whole of the Bonhoeffer upbringing: control of the emotions and doing what one conceives to be one's duty as a matter of course. It was only logical that Karl Bonhoeffer, too, did not reveal any of his grief. How deeply he was affected only became evident later, when it emerged

---

6. Ibid., 24.
7. Memoirs of Susanne Dress.
8. Bethge, Gremmels (eds.), *Dietrich Bonhoeffer. A Life in Pictures*, 42.

that for ten whole years he had been unable to continue the traditional family diary.

This time, too, he left so completely to his wife the feelings that he himself could not express that it almost proved too much for her. Paula Bonhoeffer expressed her grief in a way which the family found uncanny. For weeks on end she went to live with a friendly family in the neighborhood.

Dietrich was deeply affected by the death of his brother and by his mother's grief. The war had brought an end to an apparently sound world. The images from the "good old days" could not be put together again. Dietrich had to face the crisis and conflicts of a changed world. But for a long time he would not cease to long for the intact order of a past world.

Knowing Where
One Stands

───────────── 1919–1923 ─────────────

O N 24 JUNE 1922 THE PUPILS IN THE GRUNEWALD HIGH
school heard shots from the neighboring Königsallee.
Soon afterwards, they learned that Walther Rathenau, the Foreign Minister of the Weimar Republic, had been shot dead by
members of the extreme right-wing organization Consul. One
of the pupils was the seventeen-year-old Dietrich. A fellow
pupil reported his reaction: "I still remember my friend Bonhoeffer's passionate indignation. I remember his asking what
would become of Germany if its best leaders were killed. I
remember it because I was surprised at the time at its being
possible to know so exactly where one stood."[1]

In 1922 it was not easy to know where one stood. The
1919 revolution had sent the Kaiser into exile and produced the
Weimar Republic. But most people at the time felt that the
first democratic order on German soil was more like disorder.
And indeed the Republic was unstable. Supporters of the
monarchy remained in the army, the administration, and the

───────────────

1. Bethge, *Bonhoeffer*, 19.

law. Together with the new extreme right-wing groups they wanted to turn back the wheel of history. On the streets and in the factories the workers' movement was pressing for the overdue social revolution. Caught between reactionary and progressive forces, the Social Democrats and the middle-class parties found great difficulty in asserting themselves. In the social struggles they set right-wing troops against the left. Karl Liebknecht and Rosa Luxemburg were murdered by members of the Reich Corps. Their murders went unatoned: justice is blind in the right eye.

Further material for conflict came from outside. The Versailles peace treaty had dictated conditions which were felt to be unjust and ruinous by the German population. Rathenau was one of the politicians who had recognized this peace treaty. He was a realist, concerned for equilibrium and reconciliation in Europe; to the right wing, set on revenge, he was a "rubber-stamp politician," who had to be removed.

The Bonhoeffers joined in the general repudiation of the Versailles treaty. But they respected the new democratic order. The clashes of 1919 had also taken place in the family circle. Karl-Friedrich and Klaus, who as soldiers had had a taste of the social revolution outside the social structure of their family, had come home with new experiences and views. Karl-Friedrich had become a socialist: "He would like to join in the cause somehow, but Mama and Papa do not agree,"[2] Dietrich wrote to "Grandmama" in January 1919. But Mama and Papa were understanding enough to defend their "Red" against aristocratic relations in the Baltic, where uncle Rüdiger Graf von der Goltz set the troops of his former East Sea Division on the "Bolsheviks." Later, when the Bonhoeffers themselves took part

---

2. Ibid., 17.

in activities against the state, the name of the arch-conservative scourge of the Communists became the codeword for war: "Uncle Rudi has recovered a little bit, but I believe he will not do much longer,"[3] wrote Dietrich in 1942 to his sister Sabine, an exile in England.

At the beginning of the 1920s Klaus became a law student and a committed Democrat. In 1922 he wrote to his friend and later brother-in-law Hans von Dohnanyi about his fellow students in Heidelberg: "I have now got to know them politically, but when I think about it I feel sick. . . . A few days ago there was a meeting at which Professor Voetz spoke on 'The Student in the New Age,' on the basis of democratic principles. The students bawled at him, stamped their feet, and shouted personal insults. My indignation must have been very plain. At all events, I got involved in an argument with a man sitting behind me, an idiotic former lieutenant wearing a monocle. . . . It is depressing to see the people on whom one relies for the future arguing only with their eyes perpetually turned back to the 1870/71 period, and even that only in an empty pose. Hans, only think of the trouble we shall have later with these people. . . ."[4] Hans and Klaus were to become victims of Nazi justice in 1945.

Dietrich's brothers and their friends, some of whom became brothers-in-law, contributed an important insight to the family discussion: that one could not leave responsibility for developments in Germany to the anti-democratic forces. The new state needed and courted the old cultural élite, and the Bonhoeffers were open enough to take out subscriptions to new journals and to support democracy — as long as they

---

3. Letter of 17 April 1942. Bethge, *Bonhoeffer,* 660.
4. Bethge, *Bonhoeffer,* 19f.

Dietrich Bonhoeffer (right, in the middle) in his class at the Grunewald high school, about 1920 or 1921

could play a leading role in it. Beyond question they also knew where they stood, in the Republic, as well. Dietrich's brothers had successful careers, all his brothers and sisters married in keeping with their status, and he himself was the most conservative of all, an outspoken supporter of law and order, who after Rathenau's murder wrote: "A swinish people of right-wing Bolsheviks. A person like that is killed just because a stupid fool does not like him."[5]

Dietrich had a simple political view of the world. Bolshevism was disorder, the power of the streets, turning things upside down. Even in the democracy the "best leaders" came from the world to which he belonged and which was

---

5. Letter of 25 June 1922. Bonhoeffer, *Jugend und Studium*, 63f.

familiar to him. Dietrich, who up to the end of his schooldays hardly left the suburbs of south Berlin, could not understand why people went on the streets in the poor area of the north, in Wedding and Prenzlauer Berg, and wanted to change things.

Did he know where he stood? It seems rather that he knew where he came from and what he owed to his origins. More uncritically than his brothers he adopted his father's conservative views about the need for ruling élites. Karl Bonhoeffer, who succeeded in functioning undetected as a servant in his own house during a masked ball, was a privy councilor in the Republic as well, and indisputably the model for his younger son, who even more than the others had to fight for his father's recognition.

Dietrich did his best. Under his father's influence, as he described it he "turned from the phraseological to the real."[6] He sent his parents a letter from holiday: "Our director has once again set us quite stupid tasks. . . . What the trees tell me. Of course he wants dreadful phraseology. But I'm having Christel write the article, a very academic one about the anatomy and physiology of trees."[7]

That was very much along his father's lines. It is hard here to tell how much imagination and emotion Dietrich learned to suppress in himself as an adolescent. On the other hand, in the long run these capacities could not be suppressed: they sought new ways and forms of expression. One outlet was music, and another was religion. Reflections on his future career went in both directions, but at an early stage Dietrich decided to become a theologian. That is also noted in his school-leaving certificate which he was given in 1923 with the

---

6. Quoted in Gremmels and Pfeifer, *Theologie und Biographie*, 18.
7. Letter of 1 November 1920, in Bonhoeffer, *Jugend und Studium*, 30.

best marks. There was one exception: handwriting not good enough!

In their last year at school the future school-leavers were asked what they wanted to do. Dietrich also wrote up this scene later: "One day in the first form when the master asked him what he wanted to study, he quietly answered 'theology' and flushed. The boy absorbed that brief moment deep into himself. Something extraordinary had happened, and he enjoyed it and felt ashamed at the same time. . . . Now they all knew, he had told them. Now he was faced with the riddle of his life. Solemnly he stood there in the presence of his God, in the presence of his class. He was the center of attention. Did he look as he had wanted to look, serious and determined? And again he felt ashamed. For he knew about his pitiful vanity."[8]

This scene makes it clear how much his decision to study theology belongs in his conflict with his family and particularly with his father. Dietrich had found a way of being something of his own, something special. But above all he was taking the first step in departing from his father's world, of seeking his own standpoint, so as one day really to know where he stood.

---

8. Bethge, *Bonhoeffer,* 25f.

Understanding what
the Church Is

———————————— 1923–1924 ————————————

"EVERY MEAL COSTS A BILLION. I HAD TO PAY 6 BILLION for bread. Margarine costs 20 billion. I also had to pay 35 billion for university dues. Laundry is enormously expensive. One starched shirt for a few days 15 billion."[1] Dietrich began his theological studies in 1923. Despite the inflation, his parents financed him for two semesters in Tübingen. Karl had studied there, and all his sons were to begin their student days there.

Dietrich conscientiously followed in his father's footsteps. Though he was already so different from what he should be, he wanted to depart as little as possible from his father's life-style. He became a member of his father's old fraternity, the "Hedgehog." His brothers had thought fraternities old-fashioned.

Dietrich was very much the young man from a good home, a "good mixer," and already very much a man with "a lively cultural background," as fellow members of the fraternity

———————————————

1. Letters of 27 October 1923 and 3 November 1923, in Bonhoeffer, *Jugend und Studium*, 60ff.

later reported. And he did not need to bother about food and laundry. He would never learn to!

But what about the other matter, finding an identity, solving the "riddle of his life," which he hoped for from theology? Why could he now be found everywhere — except in church?

Dietrich was what one could call a religious person, but in a way which did not fit into any pattern. He did not have what the majority of theological students bring with them as a matter of course — socialization in the church. Although there were pastors in the wider family, the Bonhoeffers did not have any special link with the church. Karl Bonhoeffer's rationalism and Paula Bonhoeffer's vitality cut them off from a church in which "the mould of a thousand years lies under the gowns." In addition, the old empiricist Karl Bonhoeffer had more or less completely given up religion. "I don't understand any of it," he is said to have remarked often, with unmistakable irony. Like the indefinable world of feelings, religion was a women's matter.

Paula Bonhoeffer was deeply religious, but the erstwhile rebellious pastor's daughter did not send her children to church. She herself took over their religious education. With a picture Bible which was illustrated in the high Romantic Nazarene style of Schnorr von Carolsfeld, she introduced the children to the eventful life of the biblical stories. They made a deep impression, above all on Dietrich. He continued to read the Bible of his own accord before going to sleep, whereas Klaus smuggled his adventure stories into the cover of the Bible. The governess came from the pious Herrnhut community. She would not forbid nightly Bible readings.

Dietrich's religion was very much focused on the feelings. He distinguished between "red hymns" and "black hymns."

26

"Jesus goes before us on the way of life" was a red hymn; "Now thank we all our God" was a black hymn. Black hymns were doctrine and church, red hymns were life and faith.

Karl was not very happy about Dietrich's decision to study theology. Later he conceded that he thought Dietrich too clever for that. Theology did not enjoy a very high reputation in Berlin academic circles. It was something for people seeking to advance themselves and for those who were not up to an academic or a political career. Nor did Dietrich's brothers spare him critical commentaries. For them the church was a petty-minded, backward-looking organization. "In that case I shall reform the church," Dietrich is said to have retorted.

But now, in the first semesters of studying theology, it seemed as if he had taken on too much. From the beginning Dietrich Bonhoeffer was an outsider as a theological student. He was not at home in the church world. He was at the periphery of the world from which he came. His later friend Eberhard Bethge, who probably knew him best, said in retrospect: "Because he was lonely he became a theologian, and because he was a theologian he became lonely."[2] Dietrich was never completely integrated; in search of his own standpoint, he wandered between the worlds.

He does not seem to have been able to get beyond this point in his first two semesters at Tübingen. Theological study was only indirectly related to the existential questions which preoccupied him. The theological faculty offered history of religion, church history, and philosophy. Dietrich studied all this very much from the perspective of his middle-class cultural background. Learning and culture stood at the center, on the broadest possible basis and at the highest conceivable level. But

---

2. Bethge, *Bonhoeffer*, 23.

the problems of existence continued to press in on his unconscious.

Perhaps an accident while skating was an expression of this inner crisis. Disturbed by the way in which Dietrich kept having blackouts, his parents went to see him. They promised him a period of study in Rome.

When Dietrich set off with Klaus at the beginning of April 1924 he knew Baedeker off by heart. At the Brenner pass he wrote in his travel journal: "Imagination is beginning to turn into reality."[3]

Normally Dietrich was not a diarist. But on journeys he often wrote down his most powerful impressions. So we can still follow what happened to him on this trip. His experiences in Rome took him a great step forward.

First of all it seemed very much like a cultural adventure. "We are living in a clean house right next to the Pincio. Our hosts speak only Italian, which suits me very well." And some days later: "I got back here to find our bill, which delighted me very much because it was a third less than I had expected. . . . For joy we went into a trattoria by the Fontana Trevi and drank an excellent vino bianco and ate local cheese. Then back to the Forum, where I spent an hour in the most glorious dreams on an overturned pillar, with just the three pillars of the temple of Castor and Pollux in front of me and a good rough local wine in my stomach. All that helped towards a splendid hour which took me right back into antiquity. By then it was already 10.30; I drank another small carafe of wine with Klaus. Early mass tomorrow at St. Peter's. I'm looking forward to that very much."[4]

---

3. Italian Diary, in Bonhoeffer, *Jugend und Studium*, 81.
4. Ibid., 86ff.

Dietrich described Palm Sunday: "This morning, mass in St. Peter's presided over by a cardinal. . . . As well as the cardinal there were many others at the altar, senior clergy, seminarians, and monks. The universality of the church is fabulous: white, black, yellow all united in clerical garb under the church, but it seems very much an ideal. The palms were blessed in the great procession: big, yellow, woven branches. . . . the choir's Credo was glorious.

"On Sunday afternoon to Trinità dei Monti. It was almost indescribable. About 6 o'clock around forty young girls who wanted to become nuns were brought in a solemn procession. The organ began and they sang their vespers with great seriousness, with incredible simplicity and grace. The whole thing was so fresh, and made an unprecedented impression of the deepest piety. When the door was opened again after the brief half-hour, one had the most splendid view over the cupolas of Rome in the setting sun. Now I'm going to take a walk on the Pincio. It was a splendid day, the first day on which I gained some real understanding of Catholicism. . . . I believe I am beginning to understand the concept of the 'church.'"[5]

In Rome, church and faith, doctrine and life, which had previously been separate, came together for Dietrich. He experienced a piety which did not exclude or reject the senses. And he came to know a church which was universal and at the same time gave a binding order and a visible form to personal faith.

This insight continued to help Dietrich. At the same time he had an inkling of what was not right in his own church. "For all too long it was the refuge of the uncultured enlightenment," an association for bourgeois edification and national

---

5. Ibid., 88f.

rejoicing. Dietrich could now no longer be subject to the limitations of this church.

Later he would formulate his criticism of the church from this perspective. But to begin with, he was finally free and open to new experiences. Along with the ever-adventurous Klaus he went to Sicily; from there the two of them spontaneously took advantage of a favorable opportunity to cross to Africa for ten days.

In this phase, the idea often appears in Dietrich's journal how important it is to replace imagination with a view of reality. "You can read what you like about a country, but any idea remains as it were a painting: in the most splendid colors, but painted on a canvas at home. You need to get away from this home background, for the most glorious colors no longer to be there either, so that you stand in the East, with prejudices from home abandoned for something completely new, impossible to measure by our criteria. . . ."[6] In Tripoli this expansion of horizons became almost threatening: "It was as though in Africa enormous masses of very heavy material had been thrown into a still completely empty vessel and this vessel did not have an adequate base and threatened to break up if support did not come soon. But soon real support will be needed by thorough studies if catastrophe is not to happen; what one has seen is monstrous."[7]

Dietrich, who sought to preserve his fixed, orderly world as long as possible, sensed how what was "impossible to measure" by the criteria on which he had been brought up was threatening to throw it off the tracks. Although he was reluctant

---

6. Ibid., 97.
7. Ibid., 101.

to leave Italy, it drove him back to Berlin, to familiar ground, on which he had to work out his experiences.

His parents probably hardly suspected what had been going through his mind when at the end of his journey home from Rome he wrote: "In the last weeks so much has happened to me here which I would like to study further in much more detail. I would probably not have got round to it here, so I'm very much looking forward to Berlin again."[8]

He got back in time to register for the summer semester of 1924 in Berlin. Evidently he could only assimilate the disturbing and liberating experience of the trip by work. But his study now had a perspective. Dietrich could no longer get away from the question of what a real, living church is.

---

8. Letter of 27 May 1924, ibid., 134.

Communion of Saints

———— 1925–1927 ————

V ERY SOON AFTER HIS RETURN, IT BECAME CLEAR TO Dietrich that the Berlin of the 1920s was certainly not the place for getting firm ground under one's feet. The old order had collapsed and traditional values were being put in question. There were arguments about everything: the future of the Republic, bobbed hair for women, and the value of nudism. People were for or against the expropriation of the landed aristocracy, the new play by Bertolt Brecht, or the anti-war novel *All Quiet on the Western Front*. And in the theological faculty of the University of Berlin there was a debate on the justification for theology and the church, which until recently had been so much taken for granted.

In 1923 an article had appeared in the journal *Christian World* with the title "Fifteen Questions to the Despisers of Scientific Theology among the Theologians." In it, Adolf von Harnack, the grand old man of the Berlin Faculty, one of the authors of the Weimar constitution, and a famous church historian, claimed that the end of reason had come upon the theologians.

"If it is certain that all, that everything that is subconscious, nonrational, numinous, fascinating and so on remains subhuman as long as it is not apprehended, understood and purified by *reason,* how is it possible to wish to belittle, even reject, this reason? Is there really any other theology than that which has a firm connection and blood relationship to science in general?"[1]

The article was directed against the new Sturm und Drang movement which was spreading among the latest generation of theologians. This movement took the title of "dialectical theology"; its protagonist was Karl Barth. He owed it to himself and his community to take up the feud with Harnack:

"If theology regained the courage to be objective, the courage to become a witness of the word of revelation, of judgment, and of the love of God, then it could also be that 'science in general' would have to look out for its 'firm connection and blood relationship' to theology, rather than the other way round."[2]

Dietrich joined in this discussion body and soul. His own dilemma was portrayed in the controversy between Barth and Harnack. Harnack was Grunewald, his father's Wednesday Group of professors, middle-class humanistic learning, the reconciliation of theology with empirical science. Barth was the Swiss workers' community, the Social Democrat party, the existential question of Christian faith, the demarcation between theology, church, and bourgeois culture. One side was the Dietrich who wanted to make his academic seriousness

---

1. There is an English translation of the text of the article and Barth's reply in *The Beginning of Dialectical Theology,* ed. James M. Robinson, John Knox Press 1968, 165ff.; the quotation is on p. 166.
2. Ibid., 170.

plausible to his father and his brothers; the other was the Dietrich who in theology sought his own, different grasp of reality.

Nor was the issue just one of Dietrich's theological identity. It was the issue of what makes the church the church.

This was the question with which Karl Barth, who in the meantime had become professor in Göttingen, had terrified the German theologians. The pastor from the canton of Basel, who had grappled afresh every week with the question whether he had anything really important to say on Sunday, had arrived at the insight that only the "wholly other" Word of God can save the church. The church, said Barth, had made too many false compromises. And in order to become presentable in terms of the latest fashion, it had uncritically accepted the prevailing culture and social order and given it a religious dimension. This "culture Protestantism" had proved incapable of preventing the war and raising the social question. It represented the sort of religion which Ludwig Feuerbach had described as a human invention. With the end of the Kaiser's Reich, a church which had put so little critical distance between itself and the powerful élites of this Reich had lost a good deal of its legitimation. The only chance of a new beginning lay in reflection on the will of God attested in scripture, which stood over against human ideas of power and order.

No wonder that young theologians in Germany eagerly took up these ideas. For the church had thoroughly ruined their fathers and grandfathers. As long as the Kaiser "by God's grace" guaranteed the old order, the church did not have to worry about its right to exist. As a state church it was part of the apparatus of the ruling power, even if it had long since lost its influence on large parts of the population, above all among the workers and the critical intelligentsia. The Protestant church in particular only noticed how far it had already been marginalized after the revolution. Reactions to the loss of privileges and the movements in support of leaving the church differed. The majority of pastors longed for a return of the monarchy and voted for German nationalism. A small proportion wanted to anchor the church legally and politically in the new democratic constitution and thus safeguard its public role. Dialectical theology detected in both a false conjunction between church and state; it did not want to depoliticize the church, but to liberate it for independent action against the state as well.

Dietrich, still concerned with the quest for his own standpoint and impelled by the question of the nature of the church, was fascinated by Barth's ideas. The young theological student, barely twenty years old, was self-confident enough to defend Barth against Harnack.

"I actually had the experience of seeing a blonde young student contradicting the revered polyhistorian His Excellency von Harnack, time and again. I no longer remember just what was the subject of the discussion — though Karl Barth came into it — but I still remember the secret enthusiasm which I sensed of free, critical and independent thinking in theology,"[3] wrote a fellow student of the time in his reminiscences of Dietrich.

However, the decision for dialectical theology was again not as easy as all that. For Dietrich depended on the very world which he was attempting to put in question. More than most rooted culturally and emotionally in his family, he could not simply cast aside the middle-class involvement of the Bonhoeffers in the world. He looked for detachment but also mediation; he

-----

3. Bethge, *Bonhoeffer*, 45.

wanted both to go away and remain at the same time. It would not be until much later that Dietrich would be able to make this conflict fruitful in his theology. For the moment, he was torn between the world from which he came and the life of a theologian who puts an end to any bourgeois certainty.

First of all he attempted a compromise. It was Reinhold Seeberg, who more than anyone else represented the unholy alliance between culture Protestantism and right-wing conservatism in the faculty, to whom he reported at the beginning of the winter semester of 1925/26 for his doctoral work. The theme was *Sanctorum Communio — A Dogmatic Investigation of the Sociology of the Church.*

Sanctorum Communio is Latin for "the communion of saints," and in itself already points to the early church doctrine of the otherness, the separateness of Christians who live in the world but no longer according to its rules. Karl Barth had again drawn attention to this early Christian claim. Dietrich, too, took up the idea but added a further consideration: even if the church does not have its origin in the world, it does have a worldly social form. He noted that the church "is founded by God and yet is an empirical community like any other."[4] It must keep its distance from the world and at the same time act responsibly in it and towards it.

Young theologians tend to declare that the great conflicts in church doctrine are a thing of the past by brilliantly sketching out a "third way." Dietrich's dissertation, which was accepted by the faculty in August 1927, very much follows this line. Above all, though, it was meant to reconcile the two sides of Dietrich, the dialectical theologian and the empirical scien-

---

4. Dietrich Bonhoeffer, *Sanctorum Communio — A Dogmatic Investigation of the Sociology of the Church*, Collins and Harper and Row 1963, 32.

tist, the pious rebel and the obedient middle-class son. However, at that point of time this was of most interest to himself. He had difficulty in finding a publisher for the work. Among the theologians once again he fell between all the stools. His cousin Hans-Christoph von Hase, a theological student in Marburg, wrote to him: "Not many people will really understand it: the Barthians because of the sociology and the sociologists because of Barth."[5]

That didn't bother Dietrich. Not for the last time he had linked the theology which he was developing to the discovery of his own identity and his personal questions about existence. It would later be called "theology in the doing." What the theologian Dietrich Bonhoeffer thought was a way of coming to terms with a life-style. Connected with this is the fact that he probably never said anything that he did not also attempt to put into practice.

But what did the life of Dietrich Bonhoeffer the student look like? How did a precocious high-flyer live, while writing eight seminar papers and a dissertation in three years of study and taking an examination at an age when others were usually just beginning their studies?

"During the day I work, practice, read, and walk a good deal. Yesterday Grandmama, Suse, and I went to Fledermaus." "At present I have some very interesting work: Max Weber's sociology of religion . . . and after Weber I plan to read Troeltsch's *Social Teachings of Christian Ethics* and work right through Husserl to the end. Finally, if I still have time, I want to get to grips with Schleiermacher. All in all, it will be a very good vacation. . . ."[6]

---

5. Bethge, *Bonhoeffer*, 58f.
6. Letter of 5 August 1924, in Bonhoeffer, *Jugend und Studium*, 141.

In fact Dietrich's student life consisted almost exclusively of studying theology. There was a bit of culture and sport on the side, and also a few days walking with a fellow student "to make me rather slimmer and live up to my sisters' sense of beauty; you really get quite fat from a good deal of sitting."[7] But the other things which go to make up a student's life, the development of a personal life-style, forming new relationships outside the family, grappling with political problems, with cultural and social experiments — all that was notably absent. And at the same time Berlin was teeming with people looking for alternatives and trying out new forms of life: even the Bonhoeffer family did not remain untouched by the fact that times and morals were changing. Sabine married her Jewish friend Gerhard Leibholz, whom her parents accepted unreservedly, to the horror of their conservative relations. Moreover Sabine had declared that if they did not accept him, she would have a child by him and then they would have to.

Uncle Benedict, Paula's youngest brother, lived in Munich with a Communist painter. "He was the reason why our parents broke off their conversation when we entered the room," Susanne related.[8] She, the adventurous youngest daughter, would also sometimes drag her brothers off to parties at which people sat on cushions on the floor, smoked, and talked about God and the world. Dietrich, however, felt more at ease at the parties in the family villa, before which the domestic servants made bunches of flowers to be handed to the ladies before the dancing.

Friends and relatives were unanimous that he was a good dancer and a brilliant conversationalist. But there were also

---

7. Ibid., 142.
8. Memoirs of Susanne Dress.

occasions when he would suddenly withdraw from the hubbub and not emerge again. Many people felt drawn to him and tried to become his friend. But the friendly and popular Dietrich did not let anyone get too close to him. Outside the family there was no one whom he addressed in intimate terms. He had no close friend, and of course no girlfriend either.

Only in hints did he write later about his suffering in his periods of depression and his loneliness. But of course it was bad form in the Bonhoeffer household to express suffering and depression openly. So Dietrich was left all alone with his heavy-heartedness, and among other things he coped with it by hurling himself into work. However, during these years yet another possibility presented itself to him for overcoming isolation and allowing intimacy, albeit in an indirect way. He began to look after a Sunday school class and a youth group, with great success: the children flocked to him. When he left Berlin at the end of his study to go to Barcelona as a probationary minister, he wrote in his diary: "What affected me most was saying good-bye to the church work. . . . Pastor Meumann mentioned my name in his general prayer. For a long time church prayer has been something that has left me cold but, when the throng of children with whom I have spent two years prayed for me, the effect was incomparably greater."9

These are unusual words for someone who liked to keep his distance and only rarely expressed his feelings. Was the "communion of saints" also the place which partially at least did away with Dietrich's loneliness?

Be this as it may, he decided to take the church examination in addition to his final university examinations. For that, in addition to the usual work he also had to produce a trial

---

9. Bethge, *Bonhoeffer*, 66f.

sermon. It did not go down very well. Dietrich, who struggled all his life with sermons because he really wanted to stand by every statement, found on his report: "The writer, who is certainly driven by a powerful impulse, will have to learn to master his material; he is advised assiduously to study model sermons (Dryander, Conrad, Althaus, etc.), be careful to avoid forced or sought-after arguments, and, while seizing on whatever the most important point may be, to cultivate a simple and noble simplicity. . . ."[10]

Dietrich's father sent the report on to him in Barcelona; the old agnostic could not help making a scornful remark: "We were delighted with the general tenor of the Consistory's verdict. To learn the tone of the official church you will have to read many more model sermons. In my case things were quite different: Wernicke told me not to read any psychiatric literature, because it only made one stupid!"[11]

10. Ibid., 63.
11. Letter of 13 March 1928, ibid., 63f.

"The earth remains
our mother"

―――――――― 1928–1930 ――――――――

IN THE SPRING OF 1928 A CARD ARRIVED FROM DIETRICH IN
Barcelona on which a proud Spanish toreador could be seen
fighting with an equally proud Spanish bull. However, the head
of the bull-fighter looked very German. Dietrich, every inch
the tourist in Spain, had had himself photographed behind a
pictorial background and signed it, "Greetings from the
matador!" At the same time he wrote to his parents: "I cannot
truthfully say that I was as horrified by it as many people think
they ought to be because of their Central European civiliza-
tion. . . . In general a tremendous amount of emotion is
aroused among the people, and one is sucked into it. . . . Here
is a remnant of unrestricted passionate living."[1]

Dietrich owed to Superintendent Diestel, who was in
charge of the Berlin ordination candidates, the chance of serv-
ing as a probationary minister in Spain. Diestel had ecumenical
leanings — which meant something at that time — and had a

―――――――――――――

1. Letter of 11 April 1928. Bethge, *Bonhoeffer,* 73.

41

host of international church contacts. He introduced Dietrich to the German congregation in Barcelona.

On 15 February 1928 Dietrich arrived there and rented a room from two impoverished German ladies. "Dietrich is very comfortable there," wrote Klaus of his Easter visit to the house, "though everything is terribly primitive. The only place for everyone to wash is the toilet, which is very like a third-class lavatory on a train, except that it doesn't shake."[2]

Three years before the proclamation of the Republic and five years before the outbreak of the Civil War, Spain was a country which was still living half in the Middle Ages. Here feudalism had not been overcome either socially or culturally, and the Catholic Church was still so clearly the guardian of the old order that even Dietrich observed, "I believe there is really some justification for the foolish saying that religion is the opium of the people."[3]

Against this background, Barcelona, the capital of the province of Catalonia, which tended more to look towards France, was almost a Western European metropolis. The German community living there consisted mainly of merchants and their families, who "support the church just as they do sport or the German National Party, but less actively," and a pastor who "prefers a good glass of wine and a good cigar to a bad sermon."[4]

So here the inevitable practical shock awaited Dietrich. Only on very rare occasions did church work consist in theological discussion and spiritual matters; otherwise it consisted in doing the social round and satisfying those religious needs against which the Barthians had thundered so loudly.

---

2. Ibid., 70.
3. Ibid., 72.
4. Ibid., 75.

The probationary minister attempted to correct the style a little. He livened up the Sunday School and gave lectures to the congregation. But of course the congregation was not what he had imagined by the "communion of saints." The reason why Dietrich could nevertheless get something out of his work was that even as an adult he had never lost his childlike interest in people and their stories, his innocent openness to new impressions and other worlds. He was a good listener, and while keeping his well-known friendly distance allowed himself to be involved to a degree in the life stories of the members of his congregation, readily giving a hearing to all those who looked for support from the "German welfare society": "Bums, vagabonds, criminals on the run, many foreign legionaries, lion and other animal tamers who have run away from the Krone Circus on its Spanish tour, German dancers from the music hall here, German murderers on the run — all of whom tell their life story in detail."[5] All this brought him down to earth again from the heights of dialectical theology. In a lecture to the congregation, he said, "The man who would leave the earth, who would depart from the present distress, loses the power which still holds him by eternal, mysterious forces. The earth remains our mother, just as God remains our Father. . . ."[6]

But this reflection on the earth also had its difficulties. Dietrich, who had thought so much about the church, had not been very bothered hitherto about political and social ethics. So in his lecture on the "Foundations of a Christian Ethic," in a very Lutheran way he took over an attitude which was commonplace in German Protestantism and which was still to play a pernicious role. It went something like this: the world has

---

5. Letter of 7 July 1928, ibid., 76.
6. Bonhoeffer, *No Rusty Swords*, 43.

laws of its own which the church has to heed even if they do not correspond with the gospel. Here reference was made to Martin Luther, who, faced with the mixture of church and state power in the Middle Ages, had required in his doctrine of the two kingdoms and the two realms that secular power — law, politics, the economy — should not be misused for church ends and that spiritual power — preaching, community, sacraments — should not be misused for worldly ends. At the time that was an advanced position, since it implied a demand for freedom of faith and conscience and the secularization of worldly institutions. But what Luther's refined teaching later became in the Lutheran church in Germany can be reduced to the formula, "The church should preach the gospel and not get mixed up in politics."

This view, which is widespread even today, inexorably leads to leaving the alleged autonomy of the world intact. So in his lecture Dietrich, who later would think quite differently, ended up arguing for the relative right of the stronger in politics and business and asserting that while war was sin, it was unavoidable. Karl Barth would have gnashed his teeth could he have heard it. For Barth had similarly rejected any confusion of church and state, but had drawn quite the opposite conclusion. If God "does not wish to be a founder of religious history, but to be the Lord of our lives,"[7] then no sphere of life remains apart from this claim to rule, not even politics. However, the Lordship of Christ does not make use of political means of power, but remains a critical element in the face of any established human rule.

At this time, Dietrich had not followed Karl Barth that far in his thoughts. The reason may have been that his interest

---

7. Bethge, *Bonhoeffer*, 54.

44

was still very firmly centered on individual faith, essentially his own faith, and his own identity.

On 17 February 1927 Dietrich was back in Berlin. He already had in his briefcase the theme for the thesis to qualify him as a university teacher: *Act and Being — Transcendental Philosophy and Ontology in Systematic Theology.* A year later he presented the work to the theological faculty. Again it was about the question how the "wholly other," unapproachable God can be understood in faith and brought into human history. "God is not free of man but for man. Christ is the word of his freedom. God *is* there, which is to say not in eternal non-objectivity but . . . haveable, graspable in his Word within the church."[8] So here again Dietrich landed back in the concrete church — although he still had quite a distant relationship to it.

First of all, right at the beginning of his time in Berlin, he had taken care to avoid a spell at the cathedral seminary, which was obligatory for all probationary ministers, by writing this thesis. His mother had already warned him against the seminary: "It seems that they are quite cranky there, won't give people a key or let them have anything to do with other seminaries, etc. They are only allowed the wisdom on offer. . . ."[9] Superintendent Diestel, who was probably aware that he would lose his best candidate if he subjected him to pettifogging church discipline, also sprang to Dietrich's help here. So once again Dietrich could go about undisturbed in his hereditary environment.

However, in retrospect he did not regard this as uncon-

---

8. Dietrich Bonhoeffer, *Act and Being,* Collins and Harper and Row 1962, 90f.

9. Bethge, *Bonhoeffer,* 155.

ditionally positive. In fact once again he was concerned solely with theology and his theological awareness. It was no coincidence that, though in other respects he had virtually no acquaintance with contemporary literature, during this period he discovered the novels of Georges Bernanos. *The Star of Satan* and *The Renegade* depict the pastor and the saint who are torn between clerical arrogance and desperate skepticism. That was no new thing to Dietrich. His theological insight that any knowledge of God is not a human achievement but the grace of God clashed with the pride, the ability, the ambition of the young academic.

Later he himself wrote about this time: "I plunged into work in a very un-Christian way. An ambition that some noticed in me made my life difficult and robbed me of the love and trust of my fellow human beings. At that time I was terribly alone and left to myself. . . . I know that at that time I turned the doctrine of Jesus Christ into something of personal advantage for myself, for my crazy vanity. . . ."[10] He was equally critical about his "lack of interest" in the political developments of those years and in retrospect found this "really frivolous."[11]

The political events of 1929 evidently passed Dietrich by. The collapse of the New York Stock Exchange which ushered in the world economic crisis did not affect him any more than the appearances in Berlin of the newly nominated head of national propaganda for the Nazi party, Joseph Goebbels. He was not involved politically in either right-wing or left-wing groups. Nevertheless, Dietrich was not an unpolitical person. His political sympathy and antipathy also emerged in more personal gestures. He formed his first close friendship with

---

10. Letter of 27 January 1936, ibid., 154f.
11. Letter of 25 December 1932, ibid., 93.

Franz Hildebrandt, a theologian who was to be classified as a "half-Jew" under the "Aryan paragraph" in the church. It is hard to imagine now that even before 1933 such friendly relations indicated a person's political stance. That Dietrich, who hitherto had thought more in conservative terms, at any rate increasingly withdrew from the right wing, is also clear from the fact that he ostentatiously went to the services held by Pastor Günther Dehn in the Berlin suburb of Moabit — although as a pacifist and a Religious Socialist Dehn was hostile to the whole right-wing cartel.

However, it was not very clear to Dietrich what role he himself was to play in the political and church landscape. Once again he felt a certain aimlessness and disorientation — probably because he sensed that this question could not just be answered in academic reflection, apart from praxis.

On 31 July 1930 Dietrich gave his inaugural lecture at Berlin University. At twenty-four he was now the youngest assistant lecturer in theology. For the church, which also gave him only a "very good" in the second examination, he was too young to be ordained pastor. The prescribed minimum age was twenty-five, and the authorities would make no exceptions.

For Dietrich that was a real blessing. He got a grant to go to Union Theological Seminary, New York. And, as some years earlier in Rome, in an encounter with another world and another church he received decisive stimuli for the next few years.

"Who would wish unconcernedly and uncaringly to enter the promised land?"

─────────── 1930–1931 ───────────

O N 5 SEPTEMBER 1930 DIETRICH SET SAIL FOR AMERICA. THE next day he wrote to his grandmother, who often gave her grandson extra money for travel, "My cabin . . . lies deep in the belly of the ship. . . . I have already eaten two huge meals with a good appetite; I shall go on enjoying the ship as long as enjoyment is possible."[1]

Like all new arrivals, Dietrich's first view of the United States was the towering stone mountain of Lower Manhattan. When he had the skyscrapers and stone crevasses behind him, he got his second surprise. Union Theological Seminary is a new-old building in gothic style. Right next door is Harlem, the black ghetto.

Venerable though Union still looks even now, it is a relaxed place. The door of the room of the Professor of Social Ethics is always open. Students go in and out, and Professor Larry Rasmussen, the present occupant of the chair once held by Reinhold Niebuhr, personally brews coffee for visitors — that

───────────

1. Letter of 6 September 1930, Bethge, *Bonhoeffer*, 107.

48

has always been the Union style. Dietrich, now Niebuhr's most famous "student," had to get used to ever-open doors, and more than that.

The noon service at Union is taken by students from different countries. Nowadays liberation theology continues the tradition of the social gospel at Union. It is made clear that the gospel has a social form, not only in the church itself but in its political and social praxis. "Dietrich Bonhoeffer thought that it wasn't real theology," says Professor Rasmussen, "but then he lived out the theology of the social gospel himself."[2]

In fact Dietrich, who hitherto had engaged only in exalted university theology, wrote home at the beginning of his stay in New York: "There is no theology here."[3] At the end of his year of study the Saul had become a Paul: "The impression that has been made on me by today's advocates of the social gospel will leave its mark on me for a long time to come."[4]

What had happened? Dietrich, who in the United States emerged for the first time from his middle-class cultural ivory tower, here met people who embodied a social and political Christianity.

First of all, though, impressions were conflicting. In the United States, instead of just one Protestant church supported by the state and with an income from taxation, he found a mass of individual denominations and free churches, independent of the state and financed only by the voluntary giving of their members. Dietrich was taken round some of these churches and in them had to talk above all about the German

---

2. Communication to me from Professor Larry Rasmussen, 29 March 1989.

3. Bethge and Gremmels (eds.), *Dietrich Bonhoeffer. A Life in Pictures,* 74.

4. Ibid.

view of war and peace. It struck him that the white American middle class molded their church with their consciences and their pockets. Above all, though, he was shocked by the strict racial separation in American society which was accepted uncritically by the majority of the white churches. His brother Karl-Friedrich, just back from business discussions and a visiting lecture at Harvard, corresponded with Dietrich on the "negro question." He wrote: "I had the impression when I was over there that it is really *the* problem, at any rate for people with a conscience, and, when I was offered an appointment at Harvard, it was a quite basic reason for my disinclination to go to America for good, because I did not want either to enter upon that heritage myself or to hand it over to my hypothetical children. . . . At all events, our Jewish question is a joke in comparison; there cannot be many people left who maintain that they are oppressed here. . . . At any rate, not in Frankfurt. . . ."(!)[5]

In Union, people shared Dietrich's criticism. His fellow student Paul Lehmann and Paul's wife Marion, with whom a firm friendship developed, showed him the "other America." This included the political and social commitment of the church "from below" in the midst of the mass poverty of the economic depression, which was often combined with a completely untheoretical, direct understanding of the Bible as "good news for the poor." In this setting, in which in part the American Civil Rights movement was later to be found, the first beginnings of an overcoming of racial segregation developed. Reinhold Niebuhr recommended his students to read black American literature. Dietrich was deeply impressed by it.

---

5. Letter of 24 January 1931, Bethge, *Bonhoeffer,* 110.

Later he was to make his students and probationary ministers familiar with the music of black America.

First of all, however, he struck up a friendship which was still unusual even at Union at that time, with his black fellow student Frank Fisher from Harlem. Through him he got to know the ghetto at close quarters, along with the storefront churches in the slums, which even today are both places for services and self-help centers at the same time. Soon, every Sunday Dietrich was at the Abyssinian Baptist Church on 128 W 138 St: "I have heard the gospel preached in the Negro churches."[6]

What the gospel of liberation and redemption really meant was understood better in Harlem or the South Bronx than in Wall Street and the Waldorf Astoria. Anyone who attempted to survive there, with a view of the cold splendor of the banking and business center, amidst garbage and drugs, unemployment, sickness, and criminality, heard the message of the liberation of slaves with different ears from those of the inhabitants of Fifth Avenue. And at the Easter service in St. Peter's in the Bronx, in the celebration of the resurrection, people prayed not only for personal salvation but also for an overcoming of the structures which brought death.

In the churches of Harlem it became clear to Dietrich to what extent the "communion of saints" in his head was still the church of his own middle-class origins. And he suspected that the social dynamite of the gospel itself put in question the bourgeois nature of the church which was familiar to him, and did so in quite a different way from dialectical theology. But Dietrich was still far from being a religious socialist, nor was he a liberation theologian. However, a process began for him which

---

6. Bethge and Gremmels (eds.), *Dietrich Bonhoeffer. A Life in Pictures*, 76.

he was later to describe, in a few sentences, like this: "For the first time I discovered the Bible. . . . I had preached, I had seen a good deal of the Church, and talked and preached about it — but I had not yet become a Christian, but was my own master in a quite wild and unrestrained way . . . for all my loneliness, I was quite pleased with myself. Then the Bible, and above all the Sermon on the Mount, freed me from that. . . ."[7]

But all that did not just go on in Dietrich's head. As in Rome, so too in New York the atmosphere helped this highly intellectual man in his middle twenties to make a liberating personal breakthrough.

In the worship of the black communities, with no separation between intellect and gut-feeling, there was singing, praying, crying, weeping, and laughter and then more singing — and suddenly the "red" hymns of Dietrich's childhood were back. Here faith took on not only a social but also an emotional, indeed physical, dimension. For Dietrich, who had learned to control his feelings and his body, this was both liberating and confusing at the same time. At all events, he asked his friend Paul Lehmann to let no one know something that he confided only to him: that even during the week, his expeditions with an unknown goal were not to the New York sights but to prayer meetings and hymn-singing with the "red" hymns.

However, there is a second root for Dietrich Bonhoeffer's later political theology, and this too comes from that time.

Another member of Dietrich's course at Union was Jean Lasserre, a young pastor from France. Dietrich first of all projected on to him all the anti-French resentment of the patriotic German middle class — and entirely missed the mark. Jean

---

7. Letter of 27 January 1936, in Bethge, *Bonhoeffer*, 154f.

was a pacifist and thought nothing of the "gloire de la patrie": "It is impossible to be both a Christian and a nationalist. . . . Do we believe in the holy, universal church, the communion of saints? Or do we believe in the eternal mission of France?"[8]

Dietrich found this hard to swallow. He had not been quite so radically aware that the communion of saints which was so important to him also included the French. Hitherto pacifism had been remote from him: now he encountered it in the "arch-enemy," and found that it had a good theological foundation, in the Sermon on the Mount. That includes the Beatitudes on the peacemakers and the requirement to love one's enemy. Of course Dietrich, too, knew this chapter from the Gospel of Matthew. But generations of theologians had already been acutely concerned to tone down the Sermon on the Mount in a German Protestantism which was not at all pacifist. Their version ran: the Sermon on the Mount does not consist of instructions for transforming the world, but indicates the need for it to be redeemed by God, which the church proclaims in the gospel. That corresponded completely with the separation between the autonomy of the world on the one side and the gospel of personal salvation on the other which even Dietrich had advocated hitherto. Jean Lasserre would not allow this: he insisted that being a Christian meant "quite simply" following the commandments of Jesus and putting the fellowship of Christians into practice in a credible way, beyond all frontiers.

We can see how much these ideas attracted Dietrich from a letter which he wrote several years later to his brothers: "I think I know that I would really become clear and honest with myself if I really began to take the Sermon on the Mount

---

8. Jean Lasserre, *La Guerre et l'Evangile*, quoted in Bethge, *Bonhoeffer,* 113.

seriously. . . . There are things which it is worth supporting without compromise. And it seems to me that these include peace and social justice, or in fact Christ."[9]

Dietrich was to become one of the few people who were later to maintain this uncompromising attitude when their country engaged in pillage and warfare round the world.

First of all, however, here in the United States he had to abandon the image of the "good German." Dietrich was in fact very much the image of the typical German, and to some degree was one, as Paul Lehmann later related: above all in his attempt to do everything as well as possible. He had an aristocratic appearance, but there was nothing lordly about him. And later Jean Lasserre also remembered well how their friendship began — during the American screening of the German anti-war film *All Quiet on the Western Front.* The American public had reacted in a completely apolitical and emotional way and had sided with the former opponent: when French soldiers were killed, there was laughter and applause. Dietrich, who had almost certainly taken Jean with him to the cinema on purpose, was so upset that afterwards he could not do enough to make it up to him and be friendly.

At the end of their period of study the two friends went through the USA to Mexico in a decrepit Oldsmobile. In the meantime, Dietrich had spent Christmas with a fourth New York friend, the Swiss Erwin Sutz, in the German congregation in Cuba. There he gave a sermon on Moses, who was said to have seen the "promised land" but not to have been allowed to enter it. "With swarms of unemployed before our eyes, millions of children suffering throughout the world, the starving in China, the oppressed in India and in our own unhappy

---

9. *Gesammelte Schriften* III, 24f.

countries. . . . Who, thinking of all this, would wish unconcernedly and uncaringly to enter the promised land?"[10]

Dietrich would take this question and a new political awareness home with him. In June 1931 he returned to Berlin. There the post of assistant lecturer was awaiting him in the department of systematic theology, and a student chaplaincy at the Technical University.

At the Reichstag elections in September 1930 the Nazis had won 12 out of the 107 seats and no end to the economic and political crisis of the Weimar Republic was yet in sight. Klaus had written to his brother in the USA: "They are flirting with Fascism. I am afraid that, if this radical wave captures the educated classes, it will be all up with this nation of poets and thinkers."[11]

---

10. Quoted in Bethge, *Bonhoeffer*, 111.
11. Letter of 3 November 1930, ibid., 123.

*"Consider what
is on earth!"*

———————————— 1931–1932 ————————————

NOT MANY STUDENTS WENT TO THE LECTURES BY THE UN-
known young assistant lecturer Dietrich Bonhoeffer. In
the summer semester of 1932 he was lecturing on "The Nature
of the Church."

"He pointed out that nowadays we often ask ourselves
whether we still need the Church, whether we still need
God. But this question, he said, is wrong. We are the ones
who are questioned. The Church exists and God exists, and
we are asked whether we are willing to be of service, for
God needs us. What fascinated me in this man from the
very beginning was the way he saw things; he 'turned them
round,'" said Wolf-Dieter Zimmermann, who like many
leading churchmen of the post-War period was shaped by
Bonhoeffer's theology. "In the lecture-room Bonhoeffer was
very concentrated, quite unsentimental, almost dispas-
sionate, clear as crystal, with a certain rational coldness, like
a reporter." Dietrich began punctually and kept discipline:
only once did he make his students wait. When he began
twenty minutes late he said briefly, "One of my boys is

dying, and I wanted to have a last word with him. It had to be."[1]

Most of the students had meanwhile come to know who "Dietrich's boys" were. In the autumn, on the instructions of the church authorities, he had taken over a confirmation class which had run wild in the working-class suburb of Prenzlauer Berg. "It's the craziest part of Berlin, with the most difficult social and political conditions. To begin with the boys went mad. . . ." But Dietrich knew how to deal with children. He let the group riot for a few minutes and then began quietly to tell a story about Harlem. When things calmed down he ended the lesson and promised new stories for the next time. Dietrich told them Bible stories, which enthralled them. "Now there is absolute quiet, the boys see to that themselves. . . . It is quite new for them to be given anything other than learning the catechism. I constructed the whole lesson on the idea of the community. . . ."[2]

Dietrich's new "community" went beyond the social limits of the middle-class church. He himself left the Grunewald villa for the first time and rented a room with a baker called Heide at 61 Oderberger Strasse, north of the Alexanderplatz. His confirmation candidates could just drop in on them there. They learned chess and English. Dietrich went on expeditions with them and impressed them as a footballer. People recalled that at that time he looked more like a sportsman than a pastor or a scholar. Before the confirmation, at his own expense he got a bale of cloth for making confirmation suits, and with "his boys" cut the appropriate length for each of them. In this way they prepared for the service together.

---

1. Zimmermann (ed.), *I Knew Dietrich Bonhoeffer*, 60, 62, 66.
2. Letters of 25 December 1931 and 26 February 1932, *Gesammelte Schriften* I, 25ff.

Dietrich Bonhoeffer with his students, 1932

What Dietrich was attempting here was a prelude to his later idea of a "religion-less Christianity." He did not want to lure children alienated from the church back into the church, but to be with them in a completely unchurchly, unreligious kind of church. So the church was not identical with a particular religious form but was wherever people lived together in solidarity.

The confirmation sermon said: "No one shall ever deprive you of your faith, that God has in readiness for you a day and a sun and a dawn (one suspects that in the meantime Dietrich had come to know what was being sung in Prenzlauer Berg, 'Brothers, to the sun, to freedom' and 'Meet the dawn, you comrades all'), that he wishes us to see the Promised Land in which justice and peace and love prevail, because Christ prevails. . . ."[3]

The confirmation Sunday was 13 March 1932, the day of the German Presidential election. The voting was 49% for Hindenburg, 30% for Hitler, and 13% for Thälmann, the Communist candidate. The middle-class parties and the Social Democrats had supported Hindenburg, because they thought that he was the most promising candidate to defeat the radical right. The radical left warned, "Those who vote for Hindenburg vote for Hitler, those who vote for Hitler, vote for war." The parents of Dietrich's confirmation candidates voted for Thälmann.

It was virtually impossible for Dietrich himself to vote for the Communist candidate. For him the Communists were not an alternative, even if for the first time he had some understanding of socialist ideas and sympathy with them.

Meanwhile other young people "from good homes" were also feeling the same way. The dark sides of the capitalist system which were unmistakable in 1932 were also flouting middle-class humanistic ideals. What was one to think of an economic and social order in which, with six million unemployed in Germany alone, with countless hungry and freezing people, coffee was being thrown into the sea and grain burned to keep the price up?

When the newspapers reported this action, Bertolt Brecht and Hanns Eisler wrote the Ballad of the Sack-Throwers, which was popularized by Ernst Busch, the "Caruso of the barricades": "They throw the wheat into the fire, they throw the coffee in the sea, when will the sack-throwers throw the fat robbers after them . . . ?"

---

3. Bethge, *Bonhoeffer,* 170.

Such radical tones were quite alien to Dietrich. He was nearer to the "Social Workers' Group of East Berlin" which had been organized by the founder of the Christian Fellowship of Reconciliation, Friedrich Siegmund-Schultze. It was modeled on the settlement movement in the USA: young committed people formed small settlements at social flashpoints, in order to live and work with the people there. On this basis the Charlottenburg youth club was formed in the autumn; those involved were Anneliese Schnurmann, a friend of Susanne Bonhoeffer, who virtually also financed the project, and Dietrich with some of his students. The youth club sought to bring in unemployed young people from the streets and give them a place in which to meet, talk, and learn. The project was in no way tied to the church. Christians, Jews, and Socialists worked, discussed, and celebrated together — for the time that was left them.

Six months after it was founded, the youth club had to be closed because the roving commandos of the SA were on the streets. Anneliese Schnurmann was Jewish and had to leave Germany. The Communist young people for the moment disappeared into a place on the edge of the city which Dietrich's parents had "given" for youth work. Here Dietrich would attempt to help his persecuted friends as far as possible.

It is not surprising that such activity also had an effect on Dietrich's academic work. He was an utterly untypical phenomenon at the university, where most of the professors of theology had German nationalistic views and the majority of the students — including the theological students — appeared at university services in association uniforms, in full fig and with banners. "My theological origins are gradually becoming suspect here, and people have the feeling that they have nurtured a snake at their bosom,"[4] Dietrich wrote to Erwin Sutz. It was not just that he was soon regarded as a socialist and a pacifist — even his academic approach alienated people.

The assistant lecturer was experimenting with new, unfamiliar forms of "social learning." He went into the country with his students and invited them to "open evenings" — a "Bonhoeffer group" formed which not only did theology but talked about the racial conflict in the USA and the next project in the youth club. Evidently for Dietrich the question of credible Christian praxis and community was more important than his academic career. He did not want to go back into the ivory tower of pure knowledge. And he looked for people with whom to share a new form which combined theory and practice. About a third of his group were women students; that says something at a time when the proportion of female theological students was 3%. We may suppose that the combination of learning and living was particularly attractive to them. Were they able to make it clear to their fellow students — and the lecturer — that men could just as well cook as women could do theology?

But despite all this, Dietrich could not get right out of his old skin. His students felt that he was "close and remote at the same time, superior and distanced yet open and ready." And of course once again he was the "chief." He knew how dangerous that was and how he kept creating a circle in which he was the star. As he said in a lecture: "The spirit of sin has torn people from the Spirit of God and the neighbor. Now the Spirit is constantly centered on itself. Now it is the Lord of the world, but of the world which interprets and devises its 'I,' master in its self-enclosed, violated world. It sees fellow human

4. Letter of 25 December 1931, *Gesammelte Schriften* I, 24.

beings as things and God as one who satisfies its religious needs. . . ."[5] So for Dietrich radical obedience to the command of Jesus became a critical question about his own narcissism and liberation from his "self-enclosed world."

However, this idea now also had a political dimension. Dietrich did not spend much longer working out his problem of identity. When in 1932 the newly formed Papen government proclaimed the deliverance of Germany through the Christian world-view, he preached: " 'In the name of God, amen' is again to be the slogan, religion is again to be cultivated. . . . Are we really to be taken in by this 'In the name of God, amen'? Do we really believe that we shall be governed by it in our actions? That we, rich and poor, Germans and Frenchmen, will allow ourselves to be united by the name of God? Or is there not concealed behind our religious trends our ungovernable urge to power — in the name of God to do what we want, and in the name of the Christian attitude to life to stir up and play off one nationality against another?"[6]

A year earlier the annual conference of the World Alliance for Friendship between the Churches had been held in Cambridge. Dietrich had taken part in it as a member of the German youth delegation and had been elected one of the three European youth secretaries.

On 1 September 1931, the opening day of the conference, on the front page of all the German right-wing press there appeared a declaration by the two best-known German professors of theology, Paul Althaus and Emmanuel Hirsch, with the

---

5. Lecture of 31 July 1930. Quoted in Gremmels and Pfeifer, *Theologie und Biographie*, 21.

6. Bethge, *Bonhoeffer*, 176.

title "Protestant Church and International Reconciliation": "Under the cloak of peace, Germany's enemies from the World War are continuing the war against the German people. . . . In this situation, in our view there can in our opinion be no understanding between us Germans and the nations that were victorious in the World War; we can only show them that while they continue the war against us, understanding is impossible. . . ."[7]

These sentences give a good indication of the mood of the Protestant church in Germany, the representatives of which accused the World Alliance of internationalism and pacifism. That in this World Alliance Dietrich was soon also working with "Life and Work" could only confirm his reputation as an outsider in politics and the church.

Here a naive love of peace was quite alien to him. In his speeches at ecumenical conferences — London, Ciernohorské Kúpele, and Gland were the next locations — he in no way denied the conflicts which were actually there; at the same time he made it clear that these had to be solved peacefully by Christians because in Christ they were one community. The old formula "Christ existing as community" was given new concrete form: "The Christian is prohibited from any war service and any preparation for war. . . . It is impossible for love to lift up the sword against a Christian because in so doing it lifts it up against Christ."[8]

In 1932 Dietrich went beyond the national bounds of the idea of community as well as the social bounds. And he overcame the separation of gospel and politics once and for all: "Consider what is on earth. By that much will be decided today,

---

7. Ibid., 238.
8. Quoted in Gremmels and Pfeifer, *Theologie und Biographie*, 21.

whether we Christians have enough strength to bear witness to the world that we are no dreamers with our heads in the clouds. That we do not let things come and go as they are, that our faith really is not opium which leaves us content in the middle of an unjust world. But that precisely because we look to what is above we protest all the more stubbornly and deliberately on this earth."9

9. *Gesammelte Schriften* IV, 70f.

A Spoke in the Wheel

1933

ON 1 FEBRUARY 1933 DIETRICH GAVE A RADIO BROADCAST with the title "The Leader and the Individual in the Younger Generation." He had written it before Hitler's accession to power, and now, two days after the victory of the "Führer," the "Leader," it seemed to fit particularly well in the media landscape. Dietrich, who was far from having given up his inherited ideas of authority and order, attempted to provide a basis for authority and to limit it. He may also have had his own role as a star in mind: "The group is the womb of the Leader. It gives him everything, even his authority. . . . The group expects the Leader who derives from the group in this way to be the bodily incorporation of its ideal. . . . The individual knows that he is committed to the Leader in unconditional obedience."[1]

Doesn't that sound almost like the sentence from the bestseller of 1933, Hitler's *Mein Kampf,* which runs, "In the smallest matters as in the greatest, the movement represents the uncon-

---

1. Bonhoeffer, *No Rusty Swords,* 192, 194.

ditional authority of the Führer, coupled with the utmost responsibility . . . ," and would not millions of Germans recite on every possible opportunity, "Führer command, we follow!"?

Dietrich had nothing against authority and obedience as long as they served a good cause and trained people to their own "duty towards the orders of life, to father, teacher, judge, statesman." "Men, and particularly young men, will feel the need to give a Leader authority over them as long as they themselves do not feel mature, strong, responsible enough themselves to realize the claim that is placed in this authority. The Leader will have to be conscious of this clear limitation of his authority. If he understands his function in any other way than as it is rooted in fact, if he does not continually tell his followers quite clearly of the limited nature of his task and of their own responsibility, if he allows himself to surrender to the wishes of his followers, who would always make him their idol — then the image of the Leader will pass over into the image of the misleader."[2]

Here unwittingly Dietrich had already given a description of the mass hysteria now beginning, which produced a collective flight from responsibility into the cult of the Führer. For in the coming weeks and months not only a large part of the nation but also almost all the Protestant church was prostrate before the Führer.

> All hands to work, young Germany risks anew,
> Germany, the battle cry in need and death.
> The Führer calls, we loyally rejoice.
> The day before us, and our strength is God.[3]

---

2. Ibid., 197f.
3. Prolingheuer, *Kleine politische Kirchengeschichte*, 56.

Pastor Paul Humburg from the Rhineland wrote this verse to the tune of a well-known Nazi hymn, the Horst Wessel song.

In this atmosphere Dietrich's remarks about the leader who becomes the misleader were already so politically explosive that the producer cut off the broadcast before the end — allegedly because it ran over time. In fury, the next day Dietrich wrote a circular letter to all his friends and colleagues in which he pointed out "that the broadcast of the lecture was suddenly cut off at a completely inappropriate point which would give rise to misunderstanding. . . . The lecture will now be published in a daily newspaper."[4]

And in fact the lecture did appear uncut in a German newspaper. But soon the possibility even of that would be a thing of the past.

On 27 February 1933 the Reichstag was set on fire. A young and quite crazy Dutchman was arrested on the spot; he was a member of the Communist party and was now presented as evidence of a Communist conspiracy. This version soon proved quite untenable: the burning of the Reichstag suited the Nazis all too well. The very next day there appeared the "emergency decree" for the "protection of people and state." It authorized "restrictions on personal freedom, the right to free speech including freedom of the press, the right to congregate and associate, interference with the mail, telegraph, and telephone, the authorization of searches of houses and confiscations, and restrictions on property going beyond the limits determined here." This decree remained in force for the next twelve years: it was the "legal" basis for the National Socialist terror which now began.

---

4. Bethge and Gremmels (eds.), *Dietrich Bonhoeffer. A Life in Pictures,* 102.

At first, it was directed almost exclusively against the right wing. Four thousand Communist officials were arrested, and many of them were beaten to death in the cellars of the SA or shot "while escaping."

However, for the Protestant church this was no terror, but a restoration of order and deliverance from "serious danger." Under the slogan "better Brown than Red," it welcomed the destruction of the workers' movement and the persecution of all those who had long been a thorn in the flesh: "If the state exercises its office against those who undermine the foundations of state order, above all against those who with corrosive and mean words destroy marriage, cast scorn on faith, and besmirch death for the Fatherland, then it is exercising its office in the name of God."[5]

Things could hardly be put more clearly than that. The man who made this statement was the General Superintendent and later Bishop of Berlin, Otto Dibelius. He gave a sermon at the reopening of the Reichstag on 21 March 1933 which was broadcast by all the German stations — uncut! Before justifying the state terror, without mincing matters, to reassure all Protestant consciences, he gave the theological foundation for it: "When the life or death of the nation is at stake, state power must be used thoroughly and powerfully, whether abroad or at home. We have learned from Dr. Martin Luther that the church may not get in the way of legitimate state force if it is doing that to which it is called. Not even if it acts harshly and ruthlessly."[6]

Three weeks later, Dietrich gave a lecture to a group of Berlin pastors. Most of the people sitting there were certainly not

---

5. Prolingheuer, *Kirchengeschichte*, 53.
6. Ibid.

encouraged by the way in which the state was exercising its office. But they were good Lutherans, and so Dietrich first moved on tiptoe through the theme of church and state. The church has no right to appropriate to itself power over the state. But it may not keep out of politics if the state abrogates basic human rights. In this instance Dietrich mentioned three possibilities of church action towards the state: "In the first place it can ask the state whether its actions are legitimate and in accordance with its character as state, i.e., it can throw the state back on its responsibilities. Secondly, it can aid the victims of state action. The church has an unconditional obligation to the victims of any ordering of society, even if they do not belong to the Christian community (!). The third possibility is not just to bandage the victims under the wheel, but to put a spoke in the wheel itself."[7]

NB,

Dietrich gave the rest of his lecture to an almost empty room. His demand that the church must be prepared for political resistance had flabbergasted most of his audience. With this attitude, Dietrich remained alone in his church. The only ones who would have agreed with him, the Religious Socialists, were themselves already among the persecuted.

Paul Tillich, professor of theology and a Religious Socialist, had already written in 1932: "A Protestantism which is open to National Socialism and repudiates socialism is in process of once again betraying its task in the world. Apparently obedient to the statement that the kingdom of God is not of this world, it shows itself to be . . . obedient to the victorious powers and their demonry."[8] Paul Tillich was the first "Aryan" professor to be dismissed from office. He emigrated to the USA in 1933.

---

7. Bonhoeffer, *No Rusty Swords*, 221.

8. Documented in Röhm and Thierfelder (eds.), *Evangelische Kirche zwischen Kreuz und Hakenkreuz*, 19.

In the meantime his "non-Aryan" colleagues had largely fallen victim to the law on the "Reconstruction of the Civil Service." This law of 7 April 1933 meant an immediate ban on any Jewish and Communist officials. Dietrich's remarks in the lecture on "The Church and the Jewish Question" which he had given to the Berlin pastors also related to this measure. Beyond question the deprivation of rights and the persecution of the Jews which followed soon after the Nazi seizure of power were the decisive stimulus to his repudiation of the régime from the beginning and his fight against it. For now even very close friends and relatives, above all Dietrich's sister Sabine and her husband Gerhard Leibholz, were affected.

Sabine later wrote down her own experiences from this time. She reported what happened to her husband at the beginning of the summer semester of 1933; in April he had been appointed Professor of Constitutional Law in Göttingen. "Legs straddled, as only these SA men could stand, a couple of students were standing in front of the lecture hall in their tall boots and not allowing anyone to go in. 'Leibholz may not lecture, he is a Jew. The lectures will not take place.' The students obediently went home. . . . In Göttingen many people attempted to follow suit. Assistant lecturers who had got no further now saw their chance. . . . Thank God there were also some decent men among the professors. I'm thinking in particular of the theologian Walter Bauer. When one met him in the street he didn't cross to the other side — as often happened — but came up to my husband and complained about Hitler and the Nazis so loudly, since he was very hard of hearing, and so clearly that I anxiously kept giving a German glance (backwards, over both shoulders) to the right and the left. Old Örtmann, Professor of Civil Law, came to pay us a visit as soon

70

as my husband lost his post. 'Dear colleague,' he said, 'I'm ashamed to be a German.' "[9]

But such gestures of solidarity and support were exceptions, even in the Protestant church. When on 1 April 1933 Jewish businesses were boycotted throughout the Reich and Jewish citizens were mobbed and maltreated openly on the streets, a probationary minister from the Rhineland was furious that his church approved of this injustice. His superior, General Superintendent Stoltenhoff, replied to him: "I have some sympathy with the fact that the accumulated and justified ill-feeling at what has been done to us which has dominated the press, the stock exchange, the theatre, etc., is now being energetically ventilated."[10]

So Hitler did not need to fear any resistance from the Protestant church. It welcomed the "national revolution" all along the line. Most prominent in doing this was a group which had been founded in 1932 with the aim of combining Christianity and National Socialism. They named themselves "German Christians," and in their program called for a quite special Christianity for Germans "in keeping with the German spirit of Luther and heroic piety." This "Christianity" contained the complete Nazi ideology: "The fight against a Marxism which is hostile to religion and the people, and its Christian Socialist henchmen"; "Protection of the people from the unfit and the inferior," "Keep your race pure!" — these are statements from the guidelines of the German Christian movement.

Later, after 1945, prominent representatives of the German Christians would claim that they had been concerned to fight against paganism in the National Socialist movement and had

***

9. Leibholz-Bonhoeffer, *Vergangen*, 98f.
10. Bethge, *Bonhoeffer*, 322.

71

seized the chance of a broadly-based popular mission. Only in this way could the church once more gain respect among the unchurched masses.

Dietrich had this attitude in view when in 1944 he wrote: "The church is the church only when it exists for others. . . . In particular, our own church will have to take the field against the vice of hubris, power worship, envy, and humbug, as the root of all evil."[11] He did not live to see how German Christians felt no guilt over the concentration camps, euthanasia programs, and genocide, and how after the end of the Nazi régime almost all of them would remain in office.

Be this as it may, in 1933 for the first time their great hour struck for the "German Christians." They had backed the right horse, and the rest of the Protestant church more or less went with them. For Hitler knew their sore point: how they had never got over their loss of power and position after the 1919 revolution. He commanded whole SA units to go to church — in uniform, of course. And in a speech on 23 March 1933 he gave the assurance that "The national government sees the two Christian confessions as the most important factors in preserving our character as a people."

At last one was someone again! At last the churches were full again! And on "Potsdam Day," 21 March 1933, when the new Reich government established itself in the garrison church, had not Hitler politely bowed at the tomb of Frederick the Great to the "old Reich President," Field Marshal Hindenburg, who was revered by all the German nationalist Protestants? All the church bells had rung out, and there was hardly a dry German Protestant eye anywhere.

On 23 July, church elections took place in the Protestant

---

11. Bonhoeffer, *Letters and Papers from Prison,* 382f.

church. On the result would depend who sat in the church governments and how church politics would turn out in the next few years.

Of course there was the German Christian list. They stood on the slogan, "Build the new church of Christ in the new state of Adolf Hitler!" All those for whom this co-ordination of church and National Socialist state went too far were on the "Gospel and Church" list. Many of them were not concerned to repudiate Hitler's policy, but to reject manifest German Christian errors. "Our attitude to the state is one of obedience and love. In this election we are concerned *only* with the church."[12] The church opposition would repeat this statement all too often in subsequent years.

Dietrich was furious at this attitude: "That is the capitulation of the church to politics!"[13] Nevertheless the "Gospel and Church" list was the only alternative, and Dietrich with his friend Franz Hildebrandt and his students hurled themselves into an almost hopeless electoral struggle. Pamphlets were written and printed — and confiscated shortly before the elections. For the Reich government interfered substantially in this electoral contest. During it Dietrich came into contact with the Gestapo for the first time. To the anxious inquiry of Siegmund-Schultze, who as a pacifist and socialist had already been forced to leave Germany, he wrote: "I have not actually been in a concentration camp, although, on the occasion of the church election, the prospect of being sent there was held out to me and my colleague by the highest police authority."[14]

On the evening before the elections Hitler made a radio

---

12. Bethge, *Bonhoeffer*, 226.
13. Zimmermann (ed.), *I Knew Dietrich Bonhoeffer*, 63.
14. Bethge, *Bonhoeffer*, 227.

broadcast. He expected that on the next day, Sunday, the forces would be elected "which in form of the German Christians have deliberately taken a stand on the ground of the National Socialist state."

The German Christians received 70% of the votes and thus occupied all the key church positions.

The sermon which Dietrich gave that day bears marks of the excitement of these weeks. The preacher who was otherwise so reserved exclaimed to the community, "Its name is decision, its name is discernment of the spirits. . . . Come, you who have been left alone, you who have lost the church, let us return to Holy Scripture, let us go forth and seek the church together. . . . Church, remain a church . . . confess, confess, confess."[15]

Dietrich included himself among those who had lost the church. The church which was now establishing itself under Reich Bishop Müller and the slogan, "One people, one Reich, one Führer, one church," was no longer his church, the "communion of saints." It was even less so when at the "Brown Synod" in Wittenberg at the beginning of September 1933, among other measures of co-ordination his provincial church also adopted the state Aryan paragraph for the Protestant church — fortified by the theological opinion provided by Professors Althaus and Hirsch, in which people and race were declared to be "ordinances of creation" appointed by God. The new church law ran: "Anyone of non-Aryan descent or married to a person of non-Aryan descent may not be called as a minister or official in the general church administration. . . ."

This and other paragraphs of the new law meant the end for numerous Jewish Christians who were active as pastors, church lawyers, nurses, or kindergarten teachers. And also for

---

15. Ibid., 228.

Franz Hildebrandt, who wanted to begin a pastorate in East Berlin with Dietrich. Dietrich thereupon also resigned his position; he no longer wanted to be a pastor in this church.

Instead of this, the two friends planned a pamphlet campaign at the National Synod to be held in Wittenberg at the end of September which was finally to decide on the new church laws.

"With the tacit approval of the new church government, at provincial synods laws are being endorsed and put into force which are contrary to Holy Scripture and the very confession of the church. Here special mention must be made of the Aryan paragraph. . . ."[16] This appeal to the National Synod, "to obey God rather than men" and to reverse the "Brown" resolutions, was signed by two thousand pastors, of course including Dietrich Bonhoeffer and Franz Hildebrandt.

Martin Niemöller was also a co-author of the appeal. An old German nationalist and former U-boat commander who had voted for the Nazis in 1933, he now founded the Pastors' Emergency League as a protest against the introduction of the Aryan paragraph in the church. Within a short period some thousand pastors had signed the pledge of the Emergency League, against the violation of the Christian confession by the Aryan paragraph in the church.

However, the National Synod was not impressed by this in any way, not even by the pamphlets which were distributed in the city and nailed to trees and house walls. At the closing service the Reich Leader of the German Christians, Joachim Hossenfelder, stood to attention and called out over Luther's tomb, "My Reich Bishop, I greet you"; Franz whispered to

---

16. Bethge and Gremmels (eds.), *Dietrich Bonhoeffer. A Life in Pictures*, 114.

Dietrich that he now believed in the doctrine of the "real rotation" of Luther's bones in his grave.[17] Meanwhile Dietrich had become quite desperate. Precisely because for him the church was the visible form of Christ on earth, he could not remain in a church which betrayed Christ. He toyed with the idea of joining a free church, but things did not look much better there. So in his church he sought a flight forward and proposed that all pastors who rejected the Aryan paragraph should resign their office. Such an action would prove successful ten years later — in Norway! In Germany a pastors' strike was quite unthinkable. And the young radical theologian who so clearly called for the separation of the true church from the perverted church, who called on the church to put a spoke in the wheel, now became a sinister figure even to his friends in the church opposition. For them, Dietrich's criticism of the National Socialist state and the Reich Church simply went too far. After all, Martin Niemöller had sent a telegram to the Führer in the name of the Pastors' Emergency League assuring him of true loyalty — out of gratitude for the resignation of Germany from the League of Nations!

In this situation, all Dietrich could think of was to withdraw. In October 1933 he took a post abroad as pastor to two German communities in London. Franz Hildebrandt was soon to follow him there: they both wanted to share the work and the stipend.

From London Dietrich wrote to Karl Barth, whom in the meantime he had come to know personally: "I felt that I was incomprehensibly in radical opposition to all my friends, that my view of matters was taking me more and more into isolation. . . . I was afraid that I would go wrong out of

---

17. Ibid., 113.

obstinacy — and I saw no reason why I should see these things more correctly, better than so many able and good pastors — and so I thought that it was probably time to go into the wilderness for a while."[18]

At the beginning of October Dietrich said good-bye to his students with the words, "We must now endure in silence, and set the firebrand of truth to all four corners of the proud German Christian edifice so that one day the whole structure may collapse."[19]

---

18. Letter of 24 October 1933, in *No Rusty Swords*, 230.
19. Bethge, *Bonhoeffer*, 252.

"Open your mouth
for the dumb"

―――――――――― 1933–1934 ――――――――――

O N 17 OCTOBER 1933 DIETRICH MOVED INTO THE MANSE OF
the German congregation in Sydenham, in the south-east
London suburb of Forest Hill: "It was rather large, uninviting
and cold. Only gas fires installed in the fireplaces heated the
rooms, and of course they could not be kept going all the time.
Cold, damp air penetrated through the windows. Thus we
mostly lived in one room, and our morning baths were often
reduced to a minimum."[1] So reported Wolf-Dieter Zimmermann, who visited his old teacher at Christmas.

On 12 November 1933 Dietrich was elected by the congregation in Sydenham and St. Paul's church in the East End
of London pastor of the two foreign congregations. In south
London he was dealing with businessmen and diplomats, and
in east London with craftsmen and shop owners. The pastor's
stipend was quite modest. Moreover Dietrich avoided having
his position confirmed by the foreign office of the "Reich
Church," since this would be tantamount to recognition by

―――――――――――――――――――

1. Zimmermann, in *I Knew Dietrich Bonhoeffer*, 77.

78

the Reich Church government. That in turn meant that he gave up any rights to old age benefits and a pension.

Dietrich could make such clear gestures because his private income gave him a degree of financial independence. His friends and his students said that in any case he was generous with money and extraordinarily free-handed. He is said once to have remarked, "I just want enough money not to have to calculate." For a long time he was hardly aware that that is in itself the privilege of quite rich people. The professor's son from the suburb of Berlin villas was able to adapt to constantly new and often very simple living conditions. But he never had to give up what was really important to him, at any rate as long as he was still a free man.

In the London manse a cheerful young community developed. Dietrich and Franz Hildebrandt had many visitors: "Usually we had a sumptuous breakfast about 11 a.m. One of us had to fetch *The Times* from which we learned, during breakfast, of the latest developments in the German church struggle. Then each of us went about his task."[2]

The two friends were excellent pianists, and Dietrich was the proud owner of a Bechstein grand piano. He had it sent to London from Berlin.

"Many evenings we spent together at home . . . theological discussions, music, debates, story-telling, all following one another, passing into one another — till 2 or 3 a.m. Everything broke forth with enormous vitality."[3] This was just what Dietrich needed after the turbulent and difficult weeks which lay behind him: time to get his breath, a pause, a space to consider and clarify, by himself and with others,

2. Ibid., 78.
3. Ibid.

what had happened and what decisions the new situation called for.

Here it was not just a matter of the dangerous situation in the church. The family was also tormented by the question what attitude they should take to the new régime. All were united in repudiating the National Socialist rule of force. But what could and should be done next?

The Bonhoeffers were not among those whom the Nazis "relieved" of this decision. They were neither left-wingers nor Jews. They were not dismissed, deprived of their rights, or arrested. They had not written any works which were banned and burned. They were not disparaged but honored. For in this state, too, they were needed: Karl Bonhoeffer, the renowned psychiatrist; Karl-Friedrich, the professor of physics; and Klaus Bonhoeffer, the legal representative of the German airline Lufthansa. So too were Dietrich's brothers-in-law Rüdiger Schleicher and Hans von Dohnanyi, counselor in the Transport Ministry and the personal assistant to Franz Gürtner, Minister of Justice, the only minister whom the Nazis took over from the Weimar Republic, to give a pretense of the independent administration of justice.

Were they to give up these positions, access to important sources of information, key posts in government, business, science, and justice? How far could they use their influence and knowledge against the Nazi régime? And where were the limits to opportunistic adaptation, to forced collaboration?

The family learned how difficult this knife edge was to walk on at this very time, in the autumn weeks of 1933. Karl Bonhoeffer had to give a psychiatric opinion on Marinus van der Lubbe, the man who was said to have set fire to the Reichstag. Dietrich's father, who believed himself to have a grasp of the world with the tools of empirical, "value-free" science, gave a purely medical, scientifically unassailable opinion, to the effect that van der Lubbe was in his right mind. Whether the psychopathic young man could have been the guilty-innocent tool of the Nazis was of no interest to him professionally. That was politics, and did not fall within the competence of the doctor. Van der Lubbe was executed on 10 January 1934.

Some people had expected a different attitude from Karl Bonhoeffer. And he himself, always so certain of his rational view of the world, may also have begun to have doubts. At all events, he conceded to his youngest son for the first time that Dietrich's way of looking at the world and coping with it was not as unimportant and insignificant as he had always thought earlier. It seems that over these years it became clear to many scientists of Karl Bonhoeffer's stamp that the question of ethical orientation, of guilt and innocence, could not be answered by empirical science alone. At all events, Dietrich the theologian was now taken increasingly seriously as a conversation partner by both his father and his brothers. He had something to offer which they now needed.

Dietrich telephoned Berlin constantly; at the Forest Hill post office they quietly gave him a "quantity rebate." Although he really had wanted to go "into the wilderness," he wanted to know from friends and relations what was going on at home. "One is close enough to want to take part in everything, and too far away for active cooperation. And during the past weeks this has made things exceptionally difficult for me,"[4] he wrote in January 1934.

In fact things were in turmoil in the Protestant church. The social conflicts were still most clearly reflected in it because it was impossible simply to ban it — as in the meantime all

---

4. Bethge, *Bonhoeffer*, 256.

parties, organizations, newspapers, and organizations which did not support the Nazi party had been banned. Certainly the German Christian church government and Reich Bishop Müller had attempted as far as possible to co-ordinate even the church, but the more vigorously the "German Christians" went at it, the wider the opposition became, even among those who really saw themselves as good citizens of the "Third Reich."

It was not just the Aryan paragraph which kept the opposition alive. On 13 November 1933 the "German Christians" organized a great rally in the Sports Palace in Berlin. The chief speaker was the student chaplain and Gauobmann Reinhold Krause, who called on the church to free itself "from the Old Testament with its Jewish morality of reward, from its stories of cattle breeders and concubines," to do away with the Jewish theology of Paul, and to believe in a "heroic Jesus." Over the next few days the Reich Bishop was showered with telegrams: "Furiously protest against the scandal of the Sports Palace rally in Berlin, demand the resignation of members of the church authorities who failed to defend the confession there. . . ."[5]

The mood at the grass roots of the church began to change. Above all the active members of the church gradually came to understand what they had bought in that "great hour of popular mission." A national state with an influential Protestant church — yes! But not the church as a subordinate organization of the National Socialist state along with the SA and the Reich Cultural Alliance. Shortly before Christmas the Reich Bishop "handed over" the whole of Protestant youth to the "Führer"; all the youth organizations were compulsorily incorporated into Hitler Youth. Some of them disbanded

---

5. Röhm and Thierfelder (eds.), *Kirche zwischen Kreuz und Hakenkreuz*, 41.

beforehand to avoid this compulsory measure. On 4 January 1934 there followed the "muzzling decree," in which any discussion of the measures of the church government was forbidden on church premises and in church papers.

The Pastors' Emergency League called on its members not to obey the Reich Bishop. On 7 January the five German pastors in London cabled to Berlin: "We endorse the declaration of the Emergency League and refuse to give Reich Bishop Müller our loyalty. . . ."

That Dietrich with his many contacts stood behind the church opposition in Germany was clear to anyone, and above all to the German church authorities. They sent Chief Consistory Councilor Heckel to London, a Lutheran theologian who soon afterwards was nominated bishop and head of the Church Department for External Affairs.

Heckel was meant to bring ecumenical relations under the control of the Reich Church government. And for this he used an argument which soon hung like a sword of Damocles over the whole church opposition. All contacts with foreign churches which were not controlled by the Reich Church government were under suspicion of treacherous intent. Moreover Dietrich soon received instructions "from now on to refrain from all ecumenical activity."[6] However, he had no intention of doing that. On the contrary, he did all he could to open the eyes of the churches abroad to the true character of the Nazi régime and its Reich Church.

But that was not so simple. Many English people found it very reassuring, for example, that in Germany a "bulwark against Bolshevism" had come into being. English clergy praised the order which prevailed in the new Germany. In so

------

6. Quoted in Bethge, *Bonhoeffer*, 292.

doing they referred to prominent German theologians and church leaders. By contrast, the unknown pastor from London was in a difficult position, and not just in England. Nevertheless he did not give up: he wanted to persuade the ecumenical movement to break with the Reich Church government.

"My dear Henriod," he wrote in April 1934 to the General Secretary of the World Alliance, "I would very much have liked to discuss the situation with you again; the slowness of ecumenical procedure is beginning to look to me like irresponsibility. A decision has got to be taken some time, and it's no good waiting indefinitely for a sign from heaven . . . in this particular case it really is now or never. Should the ecumenical movement fail to realize this, then the ecumenical movement is no longer church, but a useless organization fit only for speechifying. . . . And can there still be any doubt as to the nature of that decision? For Germany today it is the confession, as it is the confession for the ecumenical movement. We must shake off our fear of this word — the cause of Christ is at stake, and are we to be found sleeping?"[7]

Dietrich took a major step forward when he won over the Bishop of Chichester and President of the World Council for Practical Christianity, George Bell, to his cause. A friendship bound George Bell, an important ecumenical figure, to Dietrich, younger than him by twenty-three years to the day. It was to survive a great deal. George Bell, who lovingly called Dietrich and Franz "my two boys," was persuaded to publish an ecumenical pastoral letter in which the Reich Church government was accused of all that was incompatible with Christian faith: the Führer principle, terrorist measures, racial discrimination.

---

7. Ibid., 294.

This message was published on 10 May 1934, three weeks before the Synod of Barmen at which the Confessing Church was constituted.

In the Protestant understanding of the post-war period, the Confessing Church quickly came to be called the "Protestant church in resistance" and the pro-Nazi German Christians were turned into a radical marginal group. Against that, however, is the recollection of contemporaries and the recognition of church historians that the Confessing Church was in no way opposed to government policy but primarily and exclusively opposed to the heresies and violent measures of the German Christians within the church. "Had Hitler only left the church in peace and occasionally cast a grateful eye on it and not just on providence, the 'Confessing Church' would never have come into existence,"[8] claims the Berlin church historian Karl Kupisch.

At the beginning of 1934 the greater part of the church opposition attempted to fight Reich Bishop Müller and reach an understanding with Chancellor Hitler. Here a good deal was staked on the aged Hindenburg.

On 25 January 1934 Hitler held a reception in the Reich Chancellery for everyone who was anybody in the Protestant church, including the leading representatives of the opposition. The latter had consulted beforehand by telephone — and Goering's security service had tapped the line. Martin Niemöller reported: "Hermann Goering arrived — at the beginning of the reception — with a red briefcase under his arm. He walked in, stood astraddle before Hitler and said: ' . . . I would like to read out a conversation which the president of the Pastors' Emergency League, Pastor Niemöller, who

---

8. Kupisch, *Kirchengeschichte* V, 126.

is present at this meeting, had an hour and a half ago.' It was like being struck by lightning. At that time I never knew that telephones could be tapped. Of course we had discussed what we should do if we were allowed to say a word to Hitler that day. I had spoken in my usual crude way. . . ."[9]

The rest is preserved in a set of notes which the London pastors made from Heckel's account: "Niemöller's telephone conversation: 'Now Hitler is with the old man. A last drop of oil. In the palm of his hand. When he comes into the antechamber he will be given a memorandum. . . . We've worked it all out splendidly.' Hitler: 'That's quite monstrous. Rebellion. I will not allow my leadership group to be broken up. I will take all necessary steps against this rebellion.' Hitler asks for objections to the Reich Bishop. The church leaders are silent."[10]

Two days later they had rediscovered their voice. "Under the influence of the great hour when the heads of the German Evangelical Church met the Reich Chancellor," they declared, "the assembled heads of the church take a united stand behind the Reich Bishop and declare themselves willing to enforce his policies and decrees in the sense desired by him, to obviate church-political opposition to the Reich Bishop and to consolidate his authority by all available constitutional means. . . ."[11]

This loyal address was also signed by the bishops of the provincial churches which were not controlled by the German Christians: Wurm of Württemberg, Meiser of Bavaria, and Marahrens of Hanover. From now on it was clear that anyone

---

9. Martin Niemöller, in Hübner (ed.), *Unser Widerstand*, 61.
10. Bethge, *Bonhoeffer*, 405.
11. Ibid., 273.

who attacked the Reich Church government attacked the leadership of the state. For many members of the Confessing Church this became a reason for putting special stress on their political loyalty to the Führer! For others, at this point the development moved in the opposite direction: they accepted the role of enemies of the state, in which they had unexpectedly been placed.

The Confessing Synod in Barmen was composed of both these groups. It rejected the German Christian view as heresy and in six theses formulated a confession which set up the Confessing Church as a counter-program to the German Christian Reich Church: "We repudiate the false teaching that the church can and must recognize yet other happenings and powers, images and truths as divine revelation alongside this one word of God . . . as if the church can turn over the form of her message and ordinances at will or according to some dominant ideological and political convictions. . . ." Behind these statements stood none other than Karl Barth; with them he had to bid his farewell to Hitler's Germany.

The Barmen declaration did not contain any statement on political events. No consensus could have been arrived at over that. But on 31 May 1934, 138 delegates from all the provincial churches voted for a confession which made the church opposition a church and denied the ruling church government the right to represent this church.

For Dietrich that was a great relief. He had "his" church again. And he would put himself at its disposal without reservation, even if he did not share the largely unpolitical attitude of the Confessing Church. "There must in the end be a break with theological backing for restraint against state action — after all, it's just anxiety," he wrote in autumn 1934 to Erwin Sutz. " 'Open your mouth for the dumb' — who in the church is still aware that in such times this is the least demand that the Bible makes?"[12]

Dietrich was quite clear about who the dumb were for whom the church had to speak. He was one of those who experienced the first wave of emigration and tried to support emigrants from Germany as much as possible. He wrote to the USA, and asked for stipends and visas — for example for the author Armin T. Wegner, who came to London completely shattered, straight from a German concentration camp.

At the same time he urged the foreign churches in the ecumenical movement to recognize only the Confessing Church and to deny this recognition to the Reich Church. However, he found it difficult to get a hearing. Who would believe that barbarism was gradually spreading in a civilized country of Europe? And who would realize that the dispute between the Confessing Church and the German Christians was anything but theological hair-splitting? Not for the last time Dietrich, who was very well informed through his family and friends, had the experience that people did not really believe him. What he said was felt to be simply impossible. And Dietrich, the "good German," had to contradict people more and more frequently.

---

12. Bethge and Gremmels (eds.), *Dietrich Bonhoeffer. A Life in Pictures*, 127.

Ban War!

1934–1935

No one is born a hero — not even Dietrich. The months which he spent in London certainly also served to clear his mind: about his readiness to endanger himself, about how much power he had to resist, and about the cost of renouncing all middle-class security.

At the beginning of this time in London he wrote to Sabine and Gerhard Leibholz: "I'm just working on my sermon for Remembrance Sunday and am forced to keep thinking about you and those days in March." At that time Gerhard's father had died, a few days after the Nazi authorities had dismissed him as city councilor. Dietrich was to have buried him, but his superior, the General Superintendent of Berlin, had urgently dissuaded him. Dietrich had given in and had not really come to terms with his action: "It still keeps tormenting me that I did not automatically accede to your request. I confess that I no longer understand myself. How could I have been so cruelly anxious at that time? And now I feel quite dreadful, not least because this is something that one can never make good. So I must simply ask you to forgive me this weakness of that time. Now I am sure that I should have done things differently."[1]

It is not that Dietrich had now suddenly become an ascetic moralist or someone who would go to his death to improve the world. He would remain what he had always been, "a logician, aesthete, *bon viveur,*" who would prefer order, harmony, and the good life to conflict and renunciation. But he now knew that he could not live like this if he became untrue to himself. It became increasingly clear to him that he could no longer withdraw from the conflicts in his church and his country.

Karl Barth strengthened him in this. "Now, one can on no account play Elijah under the juniper tree or Jonah under the gourd" (these were prophets who like Dietrich went into the wilderness for a while); with his "upright German figure" and his theological understanding he was to return to Germany as soon as possible. "Now you must think of only one thing, that you are a German, that the house of your church is on fire, that you know enough and can say what you know well enough to be able to help, and that you must return to your post by the next ship. As things are, shall we say the ship after next?"[2]

Dietrich was to take the "next" ship when he knew the task and goal awaiting him in Germany. But that stage had not yet been reached. He used the time to sort himself out and to canvass in the ecumenical movement for the true church in Germany, the Confessing Church.

This church now slowly began to take shape. After the declaration of principles in Barmen, the Confessing commu-

---

1. Leibholz-Bonhoeffer, *Vergangen,* 100f.
2. Bonhoeffer, *No Rusty Swords,* 233, 235.

nities gradually began to organize themselves. In October 1934 the Confessing synod in the Berlin suburb of Dahlem resolved on the establishment of an emergency church government over against the Reich Church government, the "Council of Brethren of the German Evangelical Church": "We call on the Christian communities, their pastors and elders, not to accept any instructions from the present Reich Church government and its authorities and to withdraw from cooperation with those who want to continue to obey this government."

That is virtually what Dietrich had wanted to establish a whole year earlier. And now people remembered him. When the preachers' seminaries of the provincial churches were dissolved by the Reich Bishop to provide German Christian places of education for children of pastors, and "Aryan proof" was required of any probationary ministers, the Council of Brethren decided to set up its own seminaries. The young radical theologian who was also joining in from London was just the person for this uncertain and risky project: on 1 January 1935 Bonhoeffer was to be appointed Director of the preacher's seminary of Berlin-Brandenburg.

Dietrich agreed on condition that the beginning of his involvement should be postponed until March. He wanted to prepare for the new "post" in his own way.

Before that there were tasks in the community and the ecumenical movement, for example his part in preparing and organizing the ecumenical youth conference which was to take place in Fanö in August 1934.

Dietrich wrote to the representatives of the World Alliance that his collaboration would be decided by the question "whether representatives of the present Reich Church government are to take part in the conference. . . . I hope that you, too, will help us to get the ecumenical movement to state

91

openly, before it is too late, which of the two churches in Germany it is prepared to recognize."[3]

For Dietrich there was no doubt that there can be only one "communion of saints." But the World Alliance could not decide to exclude the Reich Church from the ecumenical movement; after all, it was the official church in Germany. So delegations from both churches went to Fanö, and immediately became involved in vigorous discussions. Dietrich had seen to it that "his" church was represented by capable people: some of his former students, men and women, were also there. The climax of the controversy was a "declaration of war" on the "resolutions on the church situation in Germany." It proved a success for the Confessing Church, whose concerns were essentially adopted in the resolution. The Reich Church delegation protested with a counter declaration: "It repudiates the allegation that in the German Reich the free proclamation, either verbal or written, of the gospel is imperiled and that Christian education is not provided for the young. On the contrary, it holds that the conditions prevailing generally in Germany today provide a more favorable opportunity for proclaiming the gospel than ever before."[4]

In the meantime this Germany had become a police state with press censorship, a ban on assemblies, and thousands of political prisoners. There was more or less open rearmament. General conscription was expected in the imminent future. In Fanö, Dietrich repeated what the Bonhoeffer family had feared since the transfer of power to the Nazis: "Hitler means war!"

"Pastor, what would you do if there was a war?" asked a Swedish member of the conference in a discussion in the dunes.

---

3. Letter of 4 July 1934, in Bethge, *Bonhoeffer*, 301.
4. Ibid., 308.

"I pray that God will give me the strength not to take up arms," Dietrich replied.[5]

Jean Lasserre was also among the delegates. He will have been particularly delighted with the sermon which his friend and former fellow student at Union Theological College gave at the morning service on 28 August 1934: "How does peace come about? Through a system of political treaties? Through the investment of international capital in different countries? Or through universal peaceful rearmament in order to guarantee peace? Through none of these, for the sole reason that in all of them peace is confused with safety. There is no way to peace along the way of safety. . . . Once again how will peace come? Who will call us to peace so that the world will hear, will have to hear? Only the one great ecumenical council of the holy church of Christ over all the world can speak out so that the world, though it gnash its teeth, will have to hear, so that the peoples will rejoice because the church of Christ in the name of Christ has taken the weapons from the hands of their sons, forbidden war, proclaimed the peace of Christ against the raging world."[6]

Exactly fifty years later the peace movement in the two German states would hear these words anew after the installation of new medium-range missiles in Europe and call for an ecumenical peace council. At that time Dietrich remained a "voice in the wilderness" and a prophet who above all was of no account in his own country. Jean Lasserre will have urged him to preach his bold sermon; his German friends had little understanding of such pacifist tones. And the opponents of the Reich Church were beginning to get him in their sights.

---

5. Bethge and Gremmels (eds.), *Dietrich Bonhoeffer. A Life in Pictures*, 133.
6. Ibid.

Above: *With Jean Lasserre at the conference in Fanö, August 1934*
Below: *On the beach of the island of Fanö*

In September 1934 Dietrich was back in London. There were two things that he wanted to settle before he went back to Germany: he wanted to detach the London congregations from the Reich Church government and he wanted to visit Mahatma Gandhi in India.

The first plan succeeded, though the discussions and negotiations took longer than he would have liked. At least the two congregations of Sydenham and St. Paul's refused to recognize the Reich Bishop. On 4 January 1935 the church authorities voted unanimously for disestablishment. But now it was too late for the trip to India.

The invitation from Gandhi which Dietrich had worked on had arrived at the beginning of November 1934: "With reference to your desire to share my daily life, I may say that you will be staying with me if I am out of prison. . . ."[7]

For German Protestants, the majority of whom at that time were neither prepared nor in a position to look beyond the boundaries of their country and their confession, Dietrich's travel plans were simply a curiosity: what did he want in India?

In the summer of 1934 Dietrich had heard a talk by Madeline Slade, the daughter of an English admiral. In the meantime she had taken the name of Mira Bai, had become a colleague of Gandhi's, and had found an alternative life-style in India. Gandhi and his supporters lived a non-violent life without possessions and in this freedom had developed non-violent forms of resistance which the colonial power of England had found difficult to cope with. Dietrich wanted to learn these methods of Gandhi *in situ*. At that time he still thought that this form of opposition might also be possible against the Nazi government. Moreover he had again been seized by a wander-

---

7. Ibid., 137.

lust, a longing for a strange world; unlike most of his colleagues in church and theology he was of the opinion that one can also learn something from other cultures and religions.

Dietrich found his grandmother the most understanding and supportive: at an earlier stage she had encouraged him to venture on the journey to India. The ninety-two-year-old lady was interested and encouraging. She was hardly aware that she herself was following Gandhi's methods when in April 1933 she went through the SA pickets to a Jewish shop — "I do my shopping where I want to!" At that time this strategy of "civil disobedience" could still have held up the dictatorship — if only there had been enough people who were prepared to follow it.

Dietrich wanted to learn for himself this readiness to offer non-violent resistance and if necessary to suffer for it and also to introduce it to his church. For him it was the touchstone of whether or not one took the message of the Sermon on the Mount seriously. It increasingly occupied the center of his thought. And at the same time it was what really connected him with Gandhi: Gandhi, the pious Hindu teacher, who on one occasion later described Jesus' Sermon on the Mount as the nucleus of his own teaching.

Dietrich always regretted that the proposed trip to India never came off. He was all the more concerned to use the remaining time in England to work out a standpoint and a concept for the world which awaited him in his homeland. He sketched out the first chapters of a new book: *The Cost of Discipleship* was to become a new interpretation and implementation of the Sermon on the Mount. He discussed it with friends and colleagues. He asked with a vigor which some people found unusual about the contemporary significance of its message, and he asserted the binding nature of its commands.

"If one really wanted to raise a lively discussion, one had only to touch on the subject of divorce or pacifism. His opinion against the former and in favor of the latter was so marked and clear in his mind that the discussion soon developed into an argument, presumably as we thought the opposite,"[8] remarked Lawrence B. Whitburn and his wife, whose guest Dietrich often was.

The Sermon on the Mount, which may have been a kind of "catechism" or even "basic law" of the earliest Christian community, reflects what the Jesus movement attempted to practice as an alternative form of life: non-violence, love of enemy, justice, and the fulfillment of human forms of community like friendship and marriage not by the "letter" but by the spirit of God's commands. Dietrich, who even as a child was regarded as an "intense" person, felt that this also spoke to him personally. He was not interested in half measures. That is probably also the reason why he entered into only a very few really close relationships in his life; it would have been unthinkable for him to enter into "temporary" liaisons which could have followed from his restless life-style.

For Dietrich, at this time there began a phase in life in which, as he said later, he attempted "to lead something like a holy life."[9] This idea was nothing new, for the "communion of saints," the particular form of Christian community, of living in the world, had already preoccupied him at an earlier stage. But now the question had become more radical, for the traditional form of existence of this community, the church, had collapsed where he lived — and he was to help to discover and

---

8. Lawrence B. Whitburn, in Zimmermann (ed.), *I Knew Dietrich Bonhoeffer*, 80.

9. Bonhoeffer, *Letters and Papers from Prison*, 193.

build up new forms. But how could that happen without those who wanted this new church embodying it themselves, making it visible through the whole of human existence?

Dietrich was concerned with this totality, the rejection of half measures, false concerns, and cowardly compromises. But at a time in which it was a matter of either-or, that meant saying good-bye to his middle-class security and extricating himself from relationships which got in the way of an undivided support of justice and a voluntary acceptance of a situation of persecution. It seems that Dietrich used his time in London inwardly to take a step behind the limits of middle-class life. To this degree he really did become a "saint," someone who is prepared to put himself outside society and the church if that is what God's cause requires.

Nevertheless it would be wrong to assume that this step meant renunciation and self-denial for Dietrich. Rather, he came a step closer to himself. He began to understand that biblical dialectic according to which those who lose life gain it.

Before his departure from London he wrote to Sabine and Gerhard Leibholz: "I don't want to leave — but more from very middle-class feelings of security, and these must not be taken too seriously — otherwise life is no longer worth anything and no longer brings any joy. So, here's to a speedy reunion!"[10]

---

10. Leibholz-Bonhoeffer, *Vergangen*, 103.

"Whoever knowingly separates himself from the Confessing Church separates himself from salvation"

1935–1936

THE FIRST COURSE AT THE PREACHERS' SEMINARY OF THE Confessing Church in Zingst on the Baltic began on 26 April 1935. The Council of Brethren of the Evangelical Church of the Old Prussian Union had organized it for probationary ministers from Pomerania. Two months later the course moved to its final domicile, the rooms of a private school in Finkenwalde, near Stettin, which had been closed down by the Nazis. The director of the seminary was hardly older than the candidates: Dietrich Bonhoeffer, aged twenty-nine, lecturer in theology and pastor of the Confessing Church, appointed by the Council of Brethren and financed by voluntary gifts, stipend 360 Reichsmark. At that time that was the salary of a junior official.

The Confessing Church in Prussia was an "emergency church," over against the established Reich Church government, and thus a voluntary church. It financed its activities and the training of its clergy with the contributions and gifts of its members. Anyone who wanted to support the Confessing Church was given a certificate of membership, the "red card."

Dietrich's mother, who had always been on a war footing with the traditional church, had no difficulty with this new resistance church. She got herself a "red card" and thus also infected the family.

The first Finkenwalde course did not just come with books, but with saws, hammers, brushes, and paint. The young theologians, who had refused to follow the Reich Church leadership, had to build their own counter-church themselves. They did so with enthusiasm, since most of them had experienced German Christianity in some form and knew the kind of "church" that they were turning their backs on.

Werner Koch, who was attending a course in Finkenwalde as a guest from Westphalia, had had to go on a "Course for Church Youth Work" on the instructions of the Reich Bishop. Of the forty-five probationary ministers, forty had appeared in SA or SS uniform. The flag ceremony, Hitler greeting, and National Socialist training were taken for granted.

He recalled: "A VIP visit was announced: Oberkirchenrat Leffler from the Thuringian provincial church office would give us a training lecture. His argument: Germany has experienced its new Pentecost. When Hitler came, there was a wind from heaven. The banner with the swastika which flies before all of us is the Holy Spirit; its fire, which inspires us and welds us together in a hitherto unprecedented community, is the one great miraculous community of the people which no longer knows any classes or states. What the first disciples had experienced at Pentecost and the enthusiasm which had gripped the German people today were the work of one and the same Spirit of God which we did right to call holy.

"Things went on in this style for about an hour. 'Now we can have a discussion of the lecture.' I was the first to speak and said, 'There is nothing to discuss here. I have only one thing to say. What we have heard is contrary to all three articles of the Christian faith. I can no longer be in the same church as Herr Leffler.'

"The Oberkirchenrat gasped. He had never come across such dogmatism — and in a young man too!"[1]

In this way Pastor Koch began his small personal church struggle with his German Christian teachers. And when the seminaries of the Confessing Church were opened for the "Renewal of the Pastorate" he knew from his own experience that such a renewal was urgently necessary.

The first Finkenwalde group had twenty-three members: they first set about restoring their living quarters. Those who were not very good handymen wrote begging letters.

> All of us can now be seen
> at Finkenwalde by Stettin.
> A large old house is empty there
> it is our home for work and prayer.
> Unfortunately it's all bare,
> with only the odd bed and chair.[2]

The response was substantial: churches, sympathizers, and patrons sent furniture, books, money, and crates of fruit and vegetables. In this way five groups passed through — and found that if need be one could get by without the state and church tax.

Again Dietrich saw his task as being more than just communicating specialist theological knowledge. The combination of life and teaching took on a new quality at Finkenwalde.

---

1. Koch, *Sollen wir K. wiederbeobachten?*, 78f.
2. See Bethge, *Bonhoeffer*, 348.

There was not only different church teaching — there was also the development of a new life-style. For none of the candidates who received their training from the notorious opposition theologian Dietrich Bonhoeffer could count on being a duly installed pastor of the official church. And as they could hardly know that the "thousand-year Reich" would last only twelve years, they had to be clear about their own personal perspectives.

In this way the preachers' seminary became a place of personal experience. And the director, who preferred to be called "Pastor" or "Brother Bonhoeffer," was faced with the task not only of teaching but also of guiding in confined surroundings the social life of a group of very different grown-up men with minds of their own.

Before his return from England, Dietrich had visited several monasteries and communities. From them he attempted to adopt some guidelines for the seminary: morning and evening prayer, periods of meditation and silence, and the rule that there should be no talk about a brother in his absence.

Helpful as this rule could be for a group living in a confined space — there were a dormitory, some study rooms, and a room which served as refectory, common room, and music room — the unusual demands brought protests from most candidates. They were not yet used to doing theology other than just in their heads. Dietrich, who himself was anything but hostile to reason, compelled them to become aware of both body and soul through meditation. For some people this was strange, and for some even painful. They rebelled against this "Catholicism" and made jokes about the Far-Eastern fads of the director — but he evidently had the energy to carry through both these and other things which somewhat broadened the horizons of the German probationary ministers of that time.

However, "Bonhoeffer's proposal to substitute a light meal for the heavy German lunch, with the principal meal in the evening, met with insurmountable opposition."[3]

The head of the seminary was unconventional in every respect. In good weather he abandoned teaching and went with students to the sea. He was still an outstanding sportsman, and in handball ran faster than his candidates. He organized discussion evenings and afternoon games, concerts and literature readings. He was firmly convinced that the powers of resistance which the future pastors would need for their life and work could grow only in a successful form of communal life.

For him personally, this experiment seems to have been significant in two ways. In fact to some degree in the "communion of saints" he achieved the removal of the loneliness that he looked for. "The summer of 1935 has been the fullest time of my life, both from the professional and from the human point of view,"[4] he wrote after his first semester in Finkenwalde. That was one thing; the other was a further step beyond thoughts of middle-class possessions and a striving for security. Dietrich put everything that he had, all that was important to him, at the disposal of his seminary: his library, the Bechstein grand, his records of gospel songs from the United States, the antique copper coal scuttles from Spain. He did not claim any special rights — except for a room of his own — and gave undivided attention to the course. All that not only earned him the respect of the students, but also led to a high degree of identification between them and their seminary and its leader. They would need this sense of togetherness: the first trial was already upon them.

---

3. Ibid., 350.
4. Ibid., 341.

In the summer of 1935 the Nazi government changed its policy towards the churches. Hitler acceded to the wishes of the Confessing Church by removing the most radical of the German Christians and dropping the Reich Bishop. In the last resort he did not want the dispute within the church to produce more opponents of the state than was necessary. It was well known that many representatives of the Confessing Church wanted reconciliation with the state. Hitler's concept of "pacification" was built on this. He appointed as Minister of Church Affairs a Protestant with nationalist tendencies and "honest broker," Hanns Kerrl, and he gave the task of forming church committees to the widely respected General Superintendent Wilhelm Zoellner. Moderate German Christians, representatives of the Confessing Church, and neutrals were to be on them.

Although the affirmation of "the formation of a National Socialist people on the basis of race, blood, and soil" was made in the call to collaborate with the church committees, a large part of the Confessing Church was ready for cooperation. Feeling that it had done enough for the gospel in the fight against German Christian heresies, it disbanded itself as a counter-church. It no longer called itself the Confessing Church but the Confessing Movement. Those unprepared to go along with this were regarded as a small radical minority: they were denied the right to call themselves the Confessing Church and were polemically called the Confessing Front.

Now at last the emergency church government in the Evangelical Church of the Old Prussian Union was branded an enemy of the state — and on 2 December 1935, in the Church Minister's decree "to safeguard the Evangelical Church," the preachers' seminaries which it had set up were declared illegal.

The seminary at Finkenwalde heard of this the same day from the Stettin evening paper. That Monday evening Dietrich called his course together and presented to the candidates the situation which one of them was to describe in a letter, a few days later, like this: "Everything we do here is now illegal and contrary to the law of the State. First there were the bans on newspapers and circular letters, and now copies run off on duplicating machines are forbidden. . . . The church committees are merely a screen to mask the destruction of the church."[5] And a letter from the Council of Brethren stated: "We can give you no guarantee that you will find employment, that you will receive a stipend, or that you will be recognized by any state authority. It is likely that your path from now on will be very hard."[6]

Dietrich told his candidates that they were free to go. He himself would remain even if only one of them stayed with him. All remained. And the next Finkenwalde courses were also full. But personal conflicts over the question of personal futures became more urgent, and they were bound up with the question what the church was and what it was not. The church committees claimed to have restored the "church of the people." They offered the candidates of the preaching seminaries "legalization," and thus employment as pastors, provided that they would submit to examination by the church consistory.

That meant that each individual budding pastor had to face this decision alone. For even the third and last Confessing Synod at Bad Oeynhausen in February 1936 did not take any clear stand on the matter. Rather, this synod brought about

---

5. Ibid., 413.
6. Ibid.

the final split between the wing of the former Confessing Church which was broadly ready for compromise and the small radical wing. The latter included the Councils of Brethren of the Old Prussian Union, of Oldenburg, Bremen, and Nassau-Hessen. They elected a provisional church government and thus chose the way towards an under-privileged voluntary church.

The question where the true church was now became even more urgent. For the candidates it looked like this: "What is the position of us younger brethren towards those who accept examination by the committees or are appointed to office by them? What separates us from such people, a decision of conscience or the word of God?"[7]

Not even the "Provisional Church Government" could answer this question clearly. So Dietrich did. His thesis was that there can be no communion between the church and the non-church. If the Confessing Church did not want to betray itself and sell itself, it had to maintain the resolutions of Barmen and Dahlem; and that meant a clear separation from the Reich Church committees and from the renewed attempt at seizure by the state. In this context, in an article about church community, he wrote the sentence, "Whoever knowingly separates himself from the Confessing Church separates himself from salvation."[8] This was bandied around in the very simplified form, "Those without a red card won't go to heaven!"

There was a great stir; Dietrich was accused in turn of heresy, enthusiasm, and Catholicism. He remained quite relaxed. When the dust had settled, it would be seen that he was right: "Either the Barmen Declaration was a true confession of

---

7. Ibid., 421.
8. Ibid., 430.

106

the Lord Jesus, effected through the Holy Spirit, in which case its character is one that shapes and divides the church; or it is the expression of a few theologians without binding force. . . ."[9] And to someone who thought that he could do good and right things even in the false church, Dietrich retorted, "If you board the wrong train it is no use running along the corridor in the opposite direction."[10]

"Bonhoeffer possessed what our church as a whole and we Christians in particular lack so much," said Albrecht Schönherr, a pupil of Bonhoeffer's and later presiding bishop of the East German Church Alliance. "He willed what he thought. And he thought sharply, logically."[11]

Nevertheless, not all the members of the Finkenwalde course sustained radical opposition. Regularly one of them would go "to the consistory," and have himself legalized and appointed by the church committees. The social and family pressure was too great, above all on those with less generous support. Dietrich would not approve of them, but he would understand. He was well aware of his privileges: with his social connections and his family background he would always get by somehow. But that was not the case for most of the "illegal" probationary ministers.

Dietrich once told his sister Susanne that one day he would like to be "insecure," otherwise he would not really be able to understand the others. Now he attempted, at least to a large degree, to share the "insecurity" of his candidates and make use of his privileges on their behalf. He had one of his

---

9. Ibid., 434f.

10. Albrecht Schönherr, in Zimmermann (ed.), *I Knew Dietrich Bonhoeffer*, 129.

11. Ibid.

seminary students transferred from the third class to the second class in the hospital at his own expense; he organized support for the first ones to be persecuted in the increasing confrontation between the Confessing Movement and the state. He shared his stipend with former seminarians who supported him in his work. But his most fundamental, personal sacrifice was probably the decision to renounce marriage and end a relationship with a woman who meant a lot to him and whom in "normal" times he certainly would have married.

Not much is known of this side of Dietrich's life. One reason is that the only two women with whom at different times he entered into a close relationship also attempted to some degree to protect that little that was private in Dietrich Bonhoeffer's public — and published — life.

The second reason was that there are times when personal happiness simply is not on. Bertolt Brecht, who in the 1930s sat in exile in Denmark, and later fled from country to country before the German army with his wife, his two children, and two women friends and collaborators who were in particular danger, wrote about his life at this time:

"I ate my food between the battles. I lay down to sleep among the murderers. I cherished love unheedingly and I looked on nature without patience. So passed the time that was given me on earth. . . ."[12]

After the seminaries were made illegal, Dietrich, who would have no truck with half measures, finally decided to live only for his candidates. He probably also guessed that concern for a wife and family would get in the way of that uncompromising stand which he required of himself and the future

---

12. From Bertolt Brecht, *An die Nachgeborenene*, id., *Gesammelte Werke* 9, Frankfurt am Main 1967, 724.

pastors of an underground church. He did not want to be vulnerable. And of course as one who all his life would not live in a situation with a normal income and a normal job, he did not want to burden anyone else with this lack of security. Here Dietrich's thought was thoroughly middle class: a man should marry only when he lives in secure circumstances and can feed a family!

It is far from certain whether the woman from whom he now parted expected that of him. For what Dietrich really thought and also said about the role of the woman as "man's helpmeet" — very much in keeping with conservative church male morality — formed no part of the relationship. First of all, it was unusual that she was a theologian with a doctorate and involved in the Confessing Church — at a time when most theologians in principle still rejected the "ministry of the woman theologian." Dietrich evidently did not; theological discussion and activity in church politics were an important part of their friendship. Together they signed appeals from the Confessing Church and saw to their distribution. The controversy over the rights of men and women in the church faded into the background here: "During the church struggle there was not so much reflection on the difference between men and women in the Confessing Church as a sense that they both belonged together in a common battle and on *one* front. People stood together and worked for one another — that was the urgent task."[13]

This sense of togetherness also survived long periods of separation: as Dietrich was basically always only "in transit" in Berlin, the relationship was essentially carried on through let-

---

13. From a letter of 30 November 1989 written to me by Dr. Elisabeth Bornkamm.

ters, until the situation in politics and the church led to the decision that the ways of the two should part. They agreed to destroy all their letters — to leave themselves completely open for the future. All that has been preserved is a farewell letter in which Dietrich writes about himself with rare openness: it contains those remarks which indicate his struggle with his narcissism, his academic pride, and his liberation through the Sermon on the Mount. In the letter it also becomes clear how much self-criticism went with the new attempt to lead something like a "holy life": "My calling is quite clear to me. What God will make of it I do not know. . . . There is still much disobedience in me and mixed motives in my profession. I feel my way here every day. I must follow the path. Perhaps it will not be such a long one. . . ."[14]

Over the next period, work and the communal life of Finkenwalde were the real content of Dietrich's life. Concentrating on what was really important to him, he fascinated those around him: "It is for such a life of one piece, such an example, that a young person longs,"[15] said Albrecht Schönherr; in Dietrich one met someone who was all of a piece.

But Dietrich, the rising "saint," also had his difficulties here. It would later become clear to him that with his desire to be "holy" the old narcissism was creeping back again through the back door — and with it phases of loneliness, self-doubt, and depression. The old way in which the upper-middle class distanced themselves from those who did not come from the same stable continued. Even worse, many candidates did not dream of living up to his demands on the "communion of saints." On the afternoon of Pentecost they actually went danc-

---

14. Letter of 27 January 1936, in Bethge, *Bonhoeffer*, 249.
15. Schönherr, in Zimmermann (ed.), *I Knew Dietrich Bonhoeffer*, 99.

ing in the neighboring village tavern — and had no idea why "Brother Bonhoeffer" was offended at this.

Things became easier for him when after initial difficulties he struck up with a member of the first course a close friendship which supported him over the next few years. Eberhard Bethge was the ideal supplement to Dietrich, who was often so buttoned up; his fellow students recall that Eberhard had an "infectious liveliness." He did not come from the upper-middle class and in some ways could act as an intermediary between the director and the candidates. He was different from Dietrich, but just as sovereign in his own way. Later, in the prison cell in Tegel, Dietrich described the beginning and meaning of this friendship in disguised form in the fragment of a novel. "I would rather say that at that time we first became human beings through each other. . . . The decisive thing was not what we both lost, namely our claim to stand alone in the world as demigods, but what we gained, namely human life in community with another human being."[16]

Along with Eberhard, Dietrich attempted a new social form: with three other candidates they founded the House of Brethren, a kind of Protestant community whose members committed themselves to do without possessions, to share goods, to celibacy, and to sacrifice for the cause of Christ in the world. In his book *The Cost of Discipleship,* Dietrich wrote: "The life of Jesus Christ on earth is not finished yet, for he continues to live in the lives of his followers."[17]

That this follower is not the "solitary hero" but draws his strength from solidarity with others was Dietrich's most important experience from the Finkenwalde experiment.

---

16. Bonhoeffer, *Fiction from Prison,* 122.
17. Bonhoeffer, *The Cost of Discipleship,* 274.

*The second Finkenwalde course, 1936. In the top row are
Albrecht Schönherr (left) and Eberhard Bethge (right).
In the bottom row is Werner Koch (fourth from the right).*

When the first illegal probationary ministers began their illegal service in the widely dispersed Confessing communities, a period of intensive visiting and support began: no one who offered himself as the embodiment of the true church of Christ to an uncertain future was to be left alone. When state pressure on the Confessing Movement grew, Eberhard Bethge wrote in the Finkenwalde circular letter: "Dear Brethren, Let us promise ourselves that whenever the trials over the way of the Confessing Church become too strong, we will turn to a brother who stands firmly in the Council of Brethren or to Finkenwalde. We owe this to our brotherhood."[18]

---

18. In Bethge, *Bonhoeffer*, 650.

"Only those who cry out for the Jews may sing Gregorian chant!"

1936–1938

DIETRICH CELEBRATED HIS THIRTIETH BIRTHDAY AMONG his Finkenwalde friends and candidates. He told them about Mexico and Spain, London and New York. Travel fever seized them, and a wish to go abroad together. In a short time Dietrich had got all the necessary procedures under way: the preachers' seminary was invited by the Swedish Church for a study visit from 1 to 10 March 1936. For the seminarians, who had just put their first great test behind them, that of having been made illegal, the trip to Sweden was a great encouragement. "We were amazed to discover how clearly they saw our situation and understood our attitude; above all to discover how definitely these Lutheran professors rejected the attitude of our Lutheran bishops."[1]

The students from Finkenwalde needed this kind of support. For at the Bad Oeynhausen synod the "Council of the Evangelical Lutheran Church in Germany" had been formed as a counter to the uncompromising Councils of Brethren; it

---

1. Bethge, *Bonhoeffer*, 42.

was prepared to work with the state church committees and thus rescue the privileges of a people's church and a state church. These were precisely the privileges to which the Finkenwalde students had bidden farewell: "It is no longer possible, as it was in the past, to lead a Christian life and at the same time be fully immersed in civic life." Now it was a matter of "confessing Christ and with this renouncing all the other gods of this world."[2]

That German theologians were speaking so clearly abroad again brought the Church Office for External Affairs and Bishop Heckel on the scene: "The Reich Ministry and Prussian Ministry for Church Affairs and the Church Office for External Affairs warn against Pastor Bonhoeffer because his influence is not conducive to German interests. . . . I have the strongest objections to his visit,"[3] wrote the Office of External Affairs to the German Embassy in Stockholm when they had received the news from Heckel. And Heckel used Bonhoeffer's appearance in Sweden as an occasion for finally getting rid of the inconvenient ecumenist.

"Since he may incur the charge of being a pacifist and an enemy of the state, it might well be advisable for the Provincial Church Committee clearly to dissociate itself from him and take steps to ensure that he will no longer train German theologians."[4] This denunciation — which later did not prevent the Evangelical Church in West Germany from nominating Heckel as bishop for those who had been driven out — cost Dietrich his permission to teach. He was banned from all German universities and especially from the Theolog-

2. Ibid.
3. Ibid., 423.
4. Ibid., 423f.

ical Faculty in Berlin, where he had still been giving regular lectures. His activity in Finkenwalde was not affected: there he was under neither the church nor the church committee. But when he published his famous article on "Church and Community," the Confessing Church came under fire because of him. Dietrich wrote to Erwin Sutz: "For the rest, my paper has made me the most reviled man of our persuasion. Not long ago, some sort of 'Lutheran' association even proposed that I should be removed from my teaching post in the Confessing Church. It is coming to the stage when the beast before which the idolators bow down will bear the caricature of Luther's features. . . ."[5]

The Finkenwalde seminarians increasingly became the *avant garde* in the Confessing Church; however, the young radicals and their "ringleaders" sometimes also felt this to be a burden. But the intensified pressure from outside led to even more resolute positions.

This is the background against which Dietrich's best-known book, *The Cost of Discipleship,* was written during these months. It begins with a rejection of the Lutheran position which assigns to the church the proclamation of the "pure gospel" of the grace of God and leaves the world its "autonomy." "Cheap grace is the deadly enemy of our church. . . . Grace sold on the market like cheapjack's wares, forgiveness of sin thrown away at cut prices. . . . Grace without price: grace without cost. . . . In such a church the world finds a cheap covering for its sins; no contrition is required, still less any real desire to be delivered from sin. . . . Grace alone does everything, they say, and so everything can remain as it was before. . . . There is no more fatal misunderstanding of Luther's

---

5. Letter of 24 October 1936, ibid., 431.

actions than to suppose that his rediscovery of the gospel of pure grace offered a general dispensation from the obedience to the command of Jesus."[6]

This brought Dietrich to his theme, "How can obedience to the command of Jesus be shown today?" His answer: by attempting to live according to the Sermon on the Mount without compromise. For him that was not retreat into a Christian ghetto in which one achieves a personal piety far from the world, but a basic program for an opposition church which does not allow the world to do what it wants. The Catholic theologian Tiemo Rainer Peters stresses that it is a misunderstanding of *The Cost of Discipleship* to detach it from the political context in which it came into being: *"The Cost of Discipleship* was also intended to be a program for the church and for politics. The book does not describe this policy, but inspires and initiates it."[7]

The public church repudiation of the opposition church also consolidated the Finkenwalde community. Their communal form of life together, which meant "not monastic segregation but innermost concentration for service outside," was above all to strengthen readiness to resist. It was not an aim in itself or a flight from reality, as in other groups which came into being at this time and which attempted to get over the wretchedness of church politics by retreating into new liturgical forms, religious aesthetics, meditation, and song. To these Dietrich objected, "Only those who cry out for the Jews may sing Gregorian chant."[8]

---

6. Bonhoeffer, *The Cost of Discipleship*, 35ff.

7. Tiemo Rainer Peters, *Jenseits von Radikalismus und Kompromiss*, quoted in the postscript to the German edition of *The Cost of Discipleship*, Munich 1989.

8. Bethge and Gremmels (eds.), *Dietrich Bonhoeffer. A Life in Pictures*, 133.

Not many Christians in Germany cried out for the Jews. Most Jewish pastors had already been dismissed from their posts. One of them was Ernst Flatow, of whom the Evangelical Consistory of the Rhine Province certified: "In his appearance and his nature Flatow has such manifest features which must be regarded as characteristic of people of Jewish race that it is impossible for him to work in a community."[9] He was lost track of in 1943, in the extermination camps.

From the beginning the Nazis left no doubt that the fight against Judaism in Germany was on their program. In September 1935 the Nuremberg Race Laws made the Jews citizens with no rights. The notice "No Jews" now hung in cinemas and swimming baths, in restaurants and universities. "Mixed marriages" were banned, and relationships between "Aryans" and "Jews" outlawed. Sabine Leibholz remarked, "There were times when I was nervous at any ring at the door, since now and again towards evening Jews were 'visited'; it was even said that some were driven through the streets in their nightshirts, and others were dragged away . . . people were free to do anything."[10]

At the same time the state police station in Bielefeld reported that the leading men of the Confessing Church "in principle endorse the position of the state on the Jewish question."[11] Certainly they defended mission to the Jews and the baptism of Jews, but they thought that the state "Jewish policy" against the "enemy" and "blight" on the people was justified. The attitudes of the "moderate" members of the Confessing

---

9. Hans Prolingheuer, *Ausgetan aus dem Land der Lebendigen*, 182.

10. Leibholz-Bonhoeffer, *Vergangen*, 107.

11. Ernst Klee, *"Judenrein." Protestanten und die Judenverfolgung*, a documentary film, documented in FR (no. 218), of 20 September 1989.

Movement became even clearer after their union with others in the Reich Church Committee: "Our Evangelical Church is more free of Jews than any other organization,"[12] proclaimed Bishop Wurm of Württemberg in the Stuttgart Stiftskirche in 1937.

This once again sharpened up the fronts in the church struggle. For the radicals of the "Confessing Front" were now supporting a lost cause not only within society but also in their church — and with them countless individual grass-roots Christians who without the blessing of their church were left to their own initiative to do whatever their conscience told them. They acted without any backing or protection from the church when they hid Jewish friends, supported those suffering political persecution, or prayed in church for Confessing pastors who had been arrested. Thus the radical Confessing Movement increasingly became the butt of state repression; the Confessing Church had as little to set against it as against the persecution of the Jews. The head of the Inner Mission in the Berlin suburb of Zehlendorf, Marga Meusel, called in vain for solidarity with "non-Aryan" Christians: "How can the church keep on making joyful acknowledgments of the National Socialist state which are political confessions and are directed against the life of some of its members?"[13]

Only the representatives of the radical wing of the Confessing Church who had supported the emergency church government resolved to take a stand. This would be the only official church declaration in which the violation of human rights by the Nazi state was condemned. And it would lead to the first deaths in the church struggle.

------

12. Ibid.
13. Ibid.

The handwriting of Dietrich Bonhoeffer can clearly be recognized in the statement drawn up by the Second Provisional Leadership of the Confessing Church which made this decision. It attacked not only the de-Christianization of public life in Germany but also the uncertainty of justice, state arbitrariness, and antisemitism: "If an antisemitism is forced on Christians within the framework of the national Socialist world-view which obliges them to hate Jews, they have to oppose to it the Christian command to love one's neighbor." The tone was cautious throughout, and the whole statement was formulated as a memorandum to be addressed in the first place only to Hitler in person. "What we have said in this letter to the Führer we must say as responsible ministers. The church stands in the hands of the Lord."

There was a desire to wait for a reaction from the Führer before part of the memorandum was made public as a pulpit declaration. But the reaction did not come, and the Provisional Church Government did not want to take the initiative in escalating the conflict with the state. So the publication of the memorandum in the *Basler Nachrichten* on 23 July 1936 broke like a bomb over the church struggle.

No one yet knew how the secret document had got abroad. But everyone in the Confessing Movement knew what the consequences of its publication would be. The whole of the Confessing Church was immediately associated with treason and high treason. The "Lutheran Council" finally broke with the uncompromising Councils of Brethren. And while the latter were ready to offer resistance, there was nothing they feared more than the suspicion of being "unpatriotic." They rushed head over heels to dissociate themselves from those who could have passed the memorandum on to the foreign press.

Suspicion immediately fell on the man who was looking

after one of the two copies of the document. Friedrich Weissler was a doctor of law and a Protestant Christian of Jewish descent. The Nazis had expelled him as director of the provincial court and the emergency church government had appointed him their legal adviser. Now he was head of the chancery of the provisional government and the ideal scapegoat for the Nazis. For when it proved that he was at least indirectly involved in the affair, his own people could not and would not support him any longer. After his arrest he was dismissed from the Provisional Church Government and thus made to look the guilty party.

What had really happened only gradually became clear. Two pupils of Bonhoeffer had led the way to the publication: Werner Koch, the probationary minister who some time earlier had already taken over unofficial press work for the Confessing Movement, and Ernst Tillich, who had probably copied the memorandum on his own initiative when Weissler had left it with him overnight to look at. In fact he had been supposed only to write a brief communiqué on it and pass that on. But when there was a risk that the memorandum would fall into oblivion, Tillich made its wording public. Three months later, Weissler, Tillich, and Koch were arrested, and in February 1937 they were put in Sachsenhausen concentration camp.

A week later Friedrich Weissler was dead. As a "full Jew" he was immediately separated from the two others and sent to the notorious bunker. Anyone who ended up there had little chance of remaining alive. For six days Weissler was exposed to the sadism of the SS thugs and he finally died under the boots of Blockführer Zeidler. The first martyr of the Confessing Church was a Jew.

It is not at all easy nowadays to do justice to the Confessing Church with its contradictory course between national loyalty and resistance, and also in its effort "to save what can be saved" in a terrorist state. It is as inappropriate to idealize its position as it is to make sweeping criticisms of it. Alongside all the failings in the "Weissler affair" there was also solidarity and protest.

Werner Koch's fiancée wrote to his parents from Berlin: "Pastor Asmussen took the funeral. Beforehand the Gestapo had asked, 'Do you want to hold a demonstration?' Immediately after the burial, in which a large number of pastors in gowns took part, the grave was photographed. It was then watched by the SS for fourteen days and nights. [They wanted to prevent an exhumation and conceal the real cause of death.] The pastors of the Confessing Church announced from all the pulpits that Weissler had entered the concentration camp in good health on 13 February and had died there on 19 February. Prayers were called for, for his wife and two children . . . please destroy this letter — I hope that we shall soon get news of Werner."[14]

Werner was meanwhile fighting for survival in the Sachsenhausen punishment company. The concentration camp was completely outside the law: it allegedly served for "re-education," but in fact served for extermination through work. Thousands succumbed in Sachsenhausen simply through illness and undernourishment while at the same time doing hard physical labor. The arbitrary torture and murder by the SS staff claimed countless victims. Werner Koch recalls: "As I was being taken out through the camp gate I heard two SS men behind me whispering, 'Today it's the pope's turn.' Hardly had we got to the workplace when the cry went up again, 'The pope, the lazy swine! He needs a rest! Lie him down! Put his head nicely

---

14. Koch, *Sollen wir K. wiederbeobachten?*, 182f.

on the ground.' In a flash they got two of the greens — criminal prisoners who wore a green stripe on their prison uniforms — and ordered them to shovel a great pile of sand over my head. I just thought, 'So this is what it's like to die.' I tried not to cry out, not to free myself, not even to pray. I simply let it go over me. . . ."[15] Werner Koch had a miraculous escape. An SS Sturmführer intervened at the last moment: they had been given orders to spare the "popes"; the "Weissler case" had caused too much of a stir.

Werner Koch spent almost two years in Sachsenhausen; he also owed his survival to the solidarity of his Communist comrades, who over the years of their imprisonment had formed illegal aid organizations in the camp. Koch's experiences here were like those of other Christians from the Confessing Movement. Almost all of them had feared and fought against the "Reds" without knowing a single one of them personally. Now the "Reds" took on a face and a name, and often they were the guardian angels. Friendships arose which previously had been inconceivable for both sides. Werner Koch needed this, since the Confessing Church dissociated itself from him: he had acted politically without any commission from the church.

However, the Finkenwalde students did not dream of dissociating themselves from him. They gave support to Koch and his fiancée, and not just moral support. When he was released in December 1938 Dietrich organized a holiday to help him recover, with friendly landowners in Pomerania. He investigated at length on a long car journey what things were like in a German concentration camp.

"None of my close friends asked about this as systemati-

---

15. Ibid., 197f.

With Eberhard Bethge, summer 1938

cally as Dietrich Bonhoeffer. After every answer he lapsed into silence. Sometimes it was minutes before he asked the next question. I sensed the effect it was having on him. It became clear to me that he was using all his strength to imagine how he himself would behave if he were in the same situation. He was certain that it would happen to him."[16]

In December 1938 the situation for the opposition church had become more acute. For a long time the problem had been far more than how to get an appointment. Twenty-seven former students had already spent longer or shorter periods in prison because they had read out critical statements from pulpits in the Confessing Churches.

16. Ibid., 246.

In summer 1937 the leading organs of the opposition church were destroyed. Martin Niemöller was arrested; he survived Sachsenhausen concentration camp in strict isolation — as Hitler's "personal prisoner." He himself later wrote critically about his own attitude and that of his church in the first years of the Third Reich: "When they arrested the Communists, I kept silent. I was not a Communist. When they took away the trade unionists, I did not protest. I was not a trade unionist. When it was my turn, there was no one left to protest."

In fact the organizations of the Confessing Church were the only institutions left on which the state had so far been unable to exert any influence. So on 29 August 1937 they were banned. The Finkenwalde seminary was closed by the Gestapo. The members of the House of Brethren, which was also dissolved, sent Dietrich a copy of his *The Cost of Discipleship*, which had just been published. It bore the inscription: "Thank you for two and a half years of loyal fellowship at Finkenwalde. May our way be even more a way of joyful discipleship."

The Finkenwalde work would go on: Dietrich and his closest colleagues were already involved in developing a plan for the continuation of clergy training in disguise. But that was a further step into illegality and a break with by far the larger part of the church, which had now settled down in the Nazi state. The Confessing Church was no longer an institution. It consisted only of its members. And now they were putting themselves at risk.

But danger was growing for the Jews in Germany in yet another way. Hans von Dohnanyi, who was using his position in the Ministry of Justice to warn those suffering political and racial persecution about the measures planned against them, gave the alarm. Before very long the passports of Jewish citizens would be marked with a J. Journeys abroad would be made very difficult; it was possible that the frontiers would be completely closed. For after the "Anschluss" of Austria, Hitler was now forcing the annexation of the Sudeten German areas on Czechoslovakian territory. The danger of war was growing daily — and the propaganda against the alleged "Conspiracy of International Jewry against the German Reich" was becoming more and more threatening.

Sabine and Gerhard Leibholz resolved with a heavy heart to escape to England. Their daughter Marianne recalls: "September 9 began with a gloriously sunny morning in Göttingen. Suddenly my mother came into our bedroom very quickly and said, 'We're going to Wiesbaden; you're not going to school today.' She told our nursery maid, 'Please, both children need to put on two woollen vests. . . .' I immediately knew that something very serious was up. My parents never went to Wiesbaden, nor had we ever had to put on more than one woollen vest. I thought, 'We're going.' We could take only what would fit into our car. Because we had no money abroad, every extra woollen vest that we could get over the frontier was important."[17]

So began for the Leibholzes the laborious life of refugees in London. But at least they were safe. On 9 November the synagogues in Germany were set on fire. The next day, people in Göttingen read in the newspaper: "Anyone who cannot understand this is incapable of understanding the voice of the people. We have seen how the temple of the vengeful God of the Jews has gone up in flames. . . . In view of the most recent events, in our city too there must no longer be any remembrance of a race which has raged worse than the plague among the peoples of the earth."[18]

17. Leibholz-Bonhoeffer, *Vergangen*, 113f.
18. Ibid., 122.

The Confessing Church was silent about the pogrom, which the Nazis called "Crystal Night." In any case, nothing but approval could be expected from the Reich Church. In his Bible, Dietrich underlined two sentences from a psalm: "They are burning all the houses of God in the land," and "No prophet speaks any longer." Beside them he put the date: 9 November 1938.

Two years later Dietrich wrote in a draft for a church confession of guilt which was never made: "The church was silent where she should have cried out. . . . The church confesses that she has witnessed the lawless application of brutal force, the physical and spiritual suffering of countless innocent people, oppression, hatred and murder, and that she has not raised her voice on behalf of the victims and has not found a way to hasten to their aid. She is guilty of the deaths of the weakest and most defenseless brothers of Jesus Christ."[19]

---

19. Bonhoeffer, *Ethics*, 92f.

"Come before winter!"

1939

Union theological seminary has a special room for visiting lecturers from home and abroad, "The Prophet's Chamber." In 1939 it was occupied by four theologians in succession whose nations were already preparing war against one another: they came from Japan, the USA, Canada, and Germany.

The German was Dietrich Bonhoeffer: he spent the most difficult and most tormenting weeks of his life in the Prophet's Chamber. In June 1939 he was admitted and given a teaching post for the coming semester. At the beginning of July he packed his bag again and went back to Germany on the last ship before the outbreak of war. In the Prophet's Chamber his successor found piles of cigarette butts and illegible notes. A diary has also been preserved from these weeks which indicates how much Dietrich fought with himself and his conflicting ideas and feelings.

He could not discuss his inner concerns with anyone. For his American friends, things were simple. They were glad to have been able to save Bonhoeffer just in time from Germany,

where he had so often been in danger. They had done everything possible for him to be able to live and work in the United
States for a while. Many other victims of political and racial
persecution were waiting in vain for a visa and a residence
permit. No one understood why he, of all people, did not want
to stay in the "free world" and why he wanted to go back again.
So he had to fight the battle with himself and make the decision
by himself.

First of all, he summed up the results of three years of the
church struggle in Germany. In the light of this the most
rational thing would be to go away. For not only had his
personal situation come to a head. As already in 1933, through
his radical views and actions he had become a security risk for
the Confessing Church — or better, what was left of it. There
were some among the leaders of the Confessing Church who
would breathe a sigh of relief if the inconvenient opposition
were finally at an end.

On 20 April 1939 the "Führer's Birthday" had been celebrated with special pomp. The churches, too, had excelled
themselves with loyal addresses. Even the *Young Church*, which
represented the concerns of the Confessing Church, wrote "on
the fiftieth birthday of the Führer": "Today it has become clear
to all that the figure of the Führer, battling mightily through
old worlds, looking on new things with his inner eye and
forcing them to come into being, has his place on those few
pages of world history which are reserved for the pioneers of
a new age. The German mission in the world of nations has
again been thrown into the scales of history with a powerful
and a firm hand. . . . We ask God to bless the Führer."

One special birthday gift had been devised a year earlier
by the leader of the church chancery, Herr Werner, who had
been appointed by the Minister for Church Affairs. All pastors

of the Evangelical Church were to swear an oath of loyalty to Hitler. The official law gazette stated: "In recognition that even in the service of the church only those can hold office who have unswerving loyalty to Führer, people and Reich, it is ordained that anyone called to spiritual office must affirm his loyalty with the following oath: 'I swear that I will be loyal and obedient to Adolf Hitler, the Leader of the German Reich and people. . . .'"

From Thuringia, the citadel of the German Christians, Bishop Sasse reported: "In a great historic hour, all the pastors of the Thuringian Evangelical Church, obeying an inner command, have with joyful hearts taken an oath of loyalty to Führer and Reich. . . . One God — one obedience in the faith. Hail, my Führer!"[1] At the same time, the cross on the Wartburg was replaced with a giant illuminated swastika.

The Councils of Brethren and the pastors of the Confessing Church were far from issuing such expressions of approval. However, they, too, no longer had the strength to offer common resistance to the requirement of an oath. After all, the text of the law stated clearly enough, "Anyone who refuses to swear the oath of loyalty is to be dismissed." The intention was unmistakable — with this law the insubordinate remnant of the Confessing Church was to be brought into line, isolated, and broken up.

For once, the illegal probationary clergy were in a "fortunate" position. At all events they were not subject to the church authorities, any more than was their teacher Dietrich Bonhoeffer. Of course they refused to take the oath — and in so doing made themselves unpopular with their colleagues in office.

---

1. Bethge, *Bonhoeffer*, 504.

In fact the Confessing Church was in a difficult position. Theologically, of course, there was agreement in repudiating the oath — but economics also made a contribution to church politics. Hitherto the emergency church government of the Council of Brethren had to some degree pulled through because the Confessing pastors in office continued to be paid by the church authorities. The church of the Council of Brethren could not even begin to cope with the social consequences of the dismissal of pastors in office with the financial means at its disposal. So it was agreed to give the oath.

Karl Barth wrote from Basel: "Was it possible, permissible, or necessary that this defeat should come about? Was there and is there really no one at all among you to take you back to the simplicity of the straight and narrow way? No one to beg you not to hazard the future credibility of the Confessing Church in this dreadful way?"[2]

Karl Barth's indignation was shared by Dietrich. For him, swearing the oath was a slap in the face of the young illegals who had struggled specifically to avoid a "regular pastorate." Along with a few other pastors and Councils of Brethren they formed the last "hard core" of the Confessing Church. Because they kept to the decisions of Dahlem, the establishment of an emergency church government independent of the state, and uncompromising separation from the "German Christians," they were called the "Dahlemites." This term increasingly became an insult; it stood for stubbornness, a lack of diplomacy, and a "desire for martyrdom." And Dietrich, as one of the most uncompromising, came under fire in two ways. Was it responsible for other young theologians to take the course of illegality under his influence when com-

---

2. Ibid., 506.

promise solutions were perhaps possible? And did not his request for an independent Confessing Church endanger what was still laboriously being maintained in the regular church institutions?

Dietrich replied to these questions in a circular letter to the former Finkenwalde students: "Anyone who looks solely after himself is deluded as to the community of the church. . . . To anyone who wants to make us faint-hearted and diffident in telling us that we ought at least to salvage our remaining resources, that we have been battered, questioned and locked up quite enough, we must reply that we are promising ourselves nothing at all from these resources. . . . We have not attached our hearts to organizations and institutions, not even to our own. . . . But we trust confidently that God will salvage his Word, and us with it, in his miraculous way. That is the only stock of resources on which we intend to take our stand."[3]

Those are bold words; anyone who took them seriously would land up in an underground church without financial resources. Dietrich was aware of this. He continued to organize the illegal training: he revived his seminary under the cloak of a post as auxiliary preacher with Superintendent Eduard Block in Schlawe. The probationary ministers worked with pastors who were loyal to the confession and were "collected" more or less secretly and in quite primitive conditions for training in Sigurdshof, an empty outpost in the grounds of a Pomeranian estate. The supplies of coal, kerosene, and food were often enough only for the next few days. Dietrich frequently went to Berlin to provide the "collective pastorate" with the most recent information and with provisions. Despite all the restrictions the candidates remember a "generous life-style": skating

---

3. Ibid., 517.

and skiing, literature, games, and music by candlelight when there was no kerosene.

But of course all this no longer had much to do with a respectable middle-class career as a pastor. Anxious parents asked whether it was really necessary. Dietrich's own parents were no exception. Was it not enough that Sabine and her family had already been forced to leave the country? Was it now necessary for Dietrich, too, to expose himself in such a way when his church had long been ready for compromise? Karl-Friedrich, who at one time had been far more of a political radical than his youngest brother, admonished Dietrich to take the family into account. Dietrich wrote back to him: "I am sorry if Mother is uneasy and is making others uneasy too. There is really no good reason for it. The fact that I may fare just as hundreds of people have already fared really must not worry us any more. To hold out on the church question means sacrifice. And why should anyone want to dissuade us? None of us is keen on going to prison, but if it does come to that, then we shall be ready to go — I hope so any way — as the cause is worth it. We start again at the beginning of next week."[4]

In the same tone he also asked his candidates to remain faithful to the "cause." We are again learning, he wrote, to pray the first petition of the Lord's Prayer: "Hallowed be thy name; Thy kingdom come; Thy will be done. By these we learn to forget ourselves and our personal condition and to hold them as of little account. How are we to remain steadfast as long as we remain so important to ourselves?"[5]

Dietrich had to think of all this while he was now sitting in New York. He was in safety. No one in the Confessing

---

4. Ibid., 500.
5. Circular letter of 24 June 1937, ibid., 487.

Church had wanted to hold him back. But he could not come to terms with having abandoned the young theologians whom he had so often encouraged to resist. Already from the ship he wrote to Eberhard Bethge on the reading for 8 June 1939: "Judge rightly. That I beg of you, brethren at home. I do not want to be spared in your thoughts. . . . My thoughts are split between yourselves and the future. . . . Greet all the brethren; they will be at evening prayers now."[6]

And in New York he wrote in his diary: "With all this, there is only Germany lacking, the brethren. The first lonely hours are difficult. I do not know why I am here. . . . The short prayer in which we remembered the German brethren almost overwhelmed me. . . . This inactivity, or activity, as the case may be, has really become simply unbearable to us when we think of the brethren and the precious time. The whole weight of self-reproach because of a wrong decision comes back and almost chokes me."[7]

Dietrich walked the streets of New York for hours: "If only doubt over my own way were overcome." For first of all the invitation to the U.S. had seemed like a sign from heaven. It was not just church politics which had made Dietrich's situation dangerous. In view of the threat of war he seriously considered refusing to serve in Hitler's army, and thus provoking a conflict which neither his family nor the Confessing Church seemed likely to be able to cope with.

In fact at the beginning of the war there would be two conscientious objectors who were active Protestant Christians: Hermann Stöhr of the Fellowship of Reconciliation and Martin Gauger. Both were executed without any church government

---

6. Ibid., 554.
7. Ibid.

133

even signing a petition for a reprieve. By contrast many Confessing pastors volunteered for military service; they could at last demonstrate that the Confessing Church, too, was patriotic.

The only attempt to put the stress elsewhere came once again from the Provisional Church Government, in 1938. It issued a liturgy of prayer which for all its nationalist tones repudiated the glorification of war and described war as a divine judgment. The churches were called on to pray for the preservation of peace. However, a year before the beginning of the war that was already a crime in the Nazi state. *Das Schwarze Korps,* the journal of the SS, had on its front page: "Such prayers have nothing to do with religion — they are political statements of treachery and sabotage against the resolute readiness of the people to commit themselves in the grave hours of their destiny. The security of the people makes the elimination of these criminals the duty of the state."

Once again their opponents had hit Protestant Christians at their most sensitive point: to most people the "attitude of the politicizing pastorate" was sinister and incomprehensible in the "great hour" in which the Germans from Austria and Czechoslovakia were finally coming "home to the Reich."

However, the Provisional Government became completely isolated when a letter became public which Karl Barth had written at this time to the Czech theologian Josef Hromadka which called on the Czechs to resist the threat of occupation: "Every Czech soldier who fights and suffers will be doing so for us, too, and — I say this unreservedly — he will also be doing it for the Church of Jesus, which in the atmosphere of Hitler and Mussolini must become the victim of either ridicule or extermination."[8]

---

8. Ibid., 510.

The leadership of the Confessing Church immediately dissociated itself from the "political theology with its democratic ideology, directed against our Fatherland" by its erstwhile church father Karl Barth. But that did not do it any good.

The Lutheran Council and especially the provincial bishops Meiser, Wurm, and Marahrens, mentioned above, put their signatures to an assurance that on religious and patriotic grounds they dissociated themselves from those responsible for the "declaration." The German News Bureau reported: "The Reich Minister for Church Affairs has taken immediate disciplinary action against the members of the so-called Lutheran Union of the German Evangelical Church by the blocking of stipends, with the object of dismissal from service."

No wonder that in this situation there was nothing that the Confessing Church feared more than that one of its leading members should become a conscientious objector. In this way it would finally be pushed aside in the great German nationalistic tumult. Dietrich knew this. When his age-group received call-up papers, he sought a way out. With his father's contacts he was able to avoid conscription once again. The invitation from the USA came as asked for, and everyone breathed a sigh of relief. But now, in New York, Dietrich could not feel happy about his life. "I would not have thought it possible for anyone of my age, after so many years abroad, to be so terribly homesick."[9]

But it was not homesickness in the "patriotic sense" that made Dietrich ill. He felt that he was not where he belonged in a general, existential sense. Since he had defined the meaning

---

9. Ibid., 556.

Above: *On the journey to New York on board the "Bremen," May 1939*
Below: *After his return, with his sister, Sabine Leibholz, July 1939*

of his life as discipleship of Jesus, what he would say about this was not a matter of indifference:

"We ought to be found only where He is. We can no longer, in fact, be anywhere else than where He is. Whether it is you working over there or I working in America, we are all only where He is. He takes us with him. Or have I, after all, avoided the place where He is? The place where He is for me?"[10]

The last sentence makes it clear that Dietrich was not concerned with formulating a law as to what a Christian may do in persecution and what not. He did not think it un-Christian to want to avoid persecution. He simply realized that *he* could not do so. In New York he was in safety. But he had lost everything that made up his life. On 20 June 1939 he decided to return to Germany.

On 26 June the church Bible reading was the verse with which the apostle Paul summons a fellow worker, "Come before winter!" Dietrich wrote in his diary: "That follows me around all day. It is as if we were soldiers home on leave, and going back into action regardless of what they were to expect. We cannot be released from it. Not as if we were essential, as if we were needed (by God?!), but simply because that is where our life is and because we abandon, destroy, our life if we are not back in the fight. It is not a matter of piety, but of something more vital. But the feelings through which God acts are not only the pious but also those vital ones. 'Do your best to come before winter' — it is not a misuse of scripture if I apply that to myself."[11]

On 7 July Dietrich was on board ship. Paul Lehmann, his old familiar friend from Union days, had not been able to get

10. Ibid., 554.
11. Ibid., 560.

back to New York until the day before. He tried everything to make his friend change his mind. He went down with him to the ship, in the hope of persuading him even then to turn back.

"Last day. Paul tried to keep me back. It's no good. Farewell half-past eleven," wrote Dietrich. "Since I've been on the ship my inner uncertainty has ceased."[12]

---

12. *The Way to Freedom*, 314.

The Masquerade of Evil

1940–1943

ON 17 JUNE 1940 DIETRICH WAS SITTING WITH HIS FRIEND
Eberhard Bethge in the garden of a café in Memel on the
Baltic. He had spoken at a pastors' conference on the invitation
of the Confessing Church there; in the evening he was to take
a service. Bethge recalls: "While we were enjoying the sun,
there suddenly boomed out from the café's loudspeaker the
fanfare signal for a special announcement: the message was that
France had surrendered. The people round about at the tables
could hardly contain themselves; they jumped up, and some
even climbed on the chairs. With outstretched arm they sang
'Deutschland, Deutschland über alles.' We had stood up too.
Bonhoeffer raised his arm in the regulation Hitler salute, while
I stood there dazed. 'Raise your arm! Are you crazy?' he whispered to me, and later: 'We shall have to run risks for very
different things now, but not for that salute!' "[1]

The Finkenwalde students had been amazed when they
saw their old teacher like this. Hitherto resistance in small

---

1. Bethge, *Bonhoeffer*, 585.

matters, for example a refusal to give the Hitler salute, had been a matter of honor. What had happened to Dietrich? Had he given in?

That is what the members of the Old Prussian Council of Brethren asked themselves when three weeks later Bonhoeffer asked them what the manifest historical victory of National Socialism meant for the resistance of the church. Kurt Scharf, later Bishop of Berlin-Brandenburg and a member of the West German peace movement, reported: "Heinrich Vogel, who was sitting next to me, jokingly whispered to me during Bonhoeffer's urgent speech, 'Look, our brother Bonhoeffer seems to believe in Hitler's victory in the war!' "[2] In fact so far all the Nazi opponents, from pastors to generals, believed and hoped that the war would lead to a crisis for the Nazi régime and favor a possible overthrow. Now the opposite had happened. Hitler was being celebrated as the "greatest general of all times." To attack him now would be the political suicide of the resistance movement.

Dietrich asked himself what it meant for the opponents of a criminal but successful régime to find themselves on the defensive. At this time he wrote: "The successful man presents us with accomplished facts which can never again be reversed. What he destroys cannot be restored. . . . The indictment falls silent with the passage of time, but the success remains and determines the course of history."[3]

Shocked, he faced the fact that the majority of the German people were rejoicing at the success of the nation and enjoying the fruits of the policy of conquest without asking who was paying the price. After every victory of Hitler's army, services

---

2. Scharf, *Widerstehen und Versöhnen*, 130.
3. Bonhoeffer, *Ethics*, 56f.

of thanksgiving were held in the churches. And on the belt-buckles of the soldiers, as in the time of the Kaiser, was written "God with us!" Who still wanted to go on claiming that God was on the side of the losers?

Through such provocative questions, Dietrich made it clear that now resistance could be offered only by those who were prepared to resist without any prospect of success. He himself had long since decided to do so. What looked like giving in was already a disguise. Dietrich had begun to work in the underground. But he could not reveal that to the Council of Brethren. Even the most radical among the Councils of Brethren would resolutely reject participation in a conspiracy against the leadership of the state. Even complicity meant danger. Dietrich could not and would not burden the Confessing Church, now almost eliminated, with his double life. He trod the way of political conspiracy without his church.

Hans von Dohnanyi, the husband of his sister Christine, now increasingly became his friend and conversation partner. A constitutional lawyer, Dohnanyi had a model career behind him. In the last years of the Weimar Republic he worked in the Reich Ministry of Justice as a personal assistant to a series of Ministers of Justice. In 1933 he was kept on, although he joined neither the Nazi Party nor the National Socialist Legal Union. He used his position to warn those in danger and enlighten the unsuspecting. As early as 1933 he started a secret file on Nazi crimes. All that the "insider" came to know about abuse of power, corruption, and the violation of human rights ended up in this "poison cupboard." Dohnanyi wanted to achieve two things. He wanted to win over the German military to a coup against the Nazi régime. After it the National Socialist ruling group were to be publicly put on trial, to show the true character of National Socialism. The Gestapo later judged that

Dohnanyi was "the author of the movement to remove the Führer and the brains behind it."

In 1940, Dohnanyi was working in the political department of the Abwehr, the office for spying and counter-espionage in the supreme command of the Wehrmacht. His chief was Colonel Wilhelm Canaris, who as head of the Abwehr during the war both served and fought against Hitler at the same time. No one who worked under Canaris was spared the twilight character of this role — not even Dietrich, who at the prompting of his brother-in-law acted as a courier for the Abwehr. He was to use his ecumenical contacts to communicate secret information about the plans and aims of the German resistance movement abroad to the Western nations. That was treason and high treason, but outwardly it looked more like collaboration.

To Karl Barth, who did not know the background, it all seemed very sinister: on the one hand Dietrich was still a man of the Confessing Church, persecuted by the state and banned from teaching, speaking, and writing; on the other hand he had been officially exempted from military service to work for the Abwehr, traveled with currency and courier passports through Europe, and carried on conversations on behalf of a German military department. It was one, moreover, which argued: "We work with Jews and Communists, why not also with Confessing pastors?"

In the 1930s the fronts had been quite obvious. Now it was difficult to distinguish where friend and foe were. Dietrich was clear about this himself. "Dear Herr Professor," he wrote to Basel, "at a time in which so much must be based simply on personal trust, everything is finished when mistrust emerges."[4] At any rate Dietrich could reveal his role to Karl

4. Bethge and Gremmels (eds.), *Dietrich Bonhoeffer. A Life in Pictures*, 191.

Barth. But of course it was "top secret"; in the ecumenical world he sacrificed his good reputation for the purpose of fighting effectively against the Nazi régime, i.e., by means of political and military conspiracy.

It is all too understandable that this role did not come easily to Dietrich, who was straightforward and uncompromising. At all events it was not the "holy life" that he once wanted to live. And originally he had imagined that his contribution to the resistance would take a different form. On the journey home from New York news had reached him of the death of Pastor Paul Schneider in Buchenwald concentration camp. Schneider was doomed to die after agonizing months in the torture bunker of Buchenwald because he would not make a single concession, even a tactical one, to the Nazis, either as a church pastor or as a concentration camp prisoner. For a long time Dietrich had regarded this "resistance to the blood" as the right form of resistance for him. But now everything had turned out differently. The confessor became a conspirator; instead of a halo he got dirty hands.

As always, now, too, theology became the controlling authority and the image of real life. Dietrich's "theology in the doing" never became clearer than in this last phase. In the pauses between his trips as a courier he began to work on the outlines of a Christian ethic. This book was never finished; it consists of fragments, of incomplete attempts to think through new experiences and problems theologically. Here the question kept coming up whether keeping out of political conflicts was not a matter of greater guilt than becoming involved in political action, which could not be free of guilt in cases of conflict. Discipleship of Jesus, he asserted, can also mean being guilty out of love of neighbor.

"Jesus is not concerned with the proclamation and realization of new ethical ideals; he is not concerned with himself being good. He is concerned solely with love for the real man, and for that reason he is able to enter into the fellowship of the guilt of men and to take the burden of their guilt upon himself. . . . If any man tries to escape guilt in responsibility he cuts himself off from the redeeming mystery of Christ's bearing guilt without sin and he has no share in the divine justification which lies upon this event. He sets his own personal innocence above his responsibility for men, and he is blind to the more irredeemable guilt which he incurs precisely in this. . . ."5

Dietrich wanted to impress on his church that the neutrality in political conflicts which it liked to claim ceased to be neutrality when it *de facto* tolerated existing power and prevailing injustice because it did not fight against these actively, even with force. It had become clear to him that his own ethical rigorism no longer worked; that it was too much bound up with his own personal search for perfection. Now he faced the question which was the greater guilt, that of tolerating the Hitler dictatorship or that of removing it. In particular, anyone who was not ready to kill Hitler was guilty of mass murder, whether he liked it or not.

Dietrich even went so far as to declare himself ready to make an attempt on Hitler's life. However, before that he would deliberately leave the church. He left no doubt that any use of force is and remains guilt. But he insisted that there can be situations in which a Christian must become guilty out of love of neighbor.

The church might not have been struggling with this problem at the same time, but that was not true of a large

---

5. Bonhoeffer, *Ethics,* 209f.

number of Christians who found themselves involved in resistance to the Hitler régime.

Hans Scholl, a medical student in Munich, was studying the attitude of medieval theologians to tyrannicide in a monastery library in Bavaria. The "White Rose" student resistance group had so far written and distributed pamphlets. Now it sought contact with other resistance groups and discussed the possibility of taking part in attempts at an overthrow. Dietrich and Klaus Bonhoeffer acted as contacts. But the conversation did not take place. The Munich group came to grief in a pamphlet campaign; its members were condemned to death after a hasty trial. Even after the war there were chaplains who dissociated themselves from commemorations of Hans and Sophie Scholl and their friends: the church had nothing to do with enemies of the state and revolutionaries!

Christians in resistance had to face all by themselves the question what guilt they were ready to shoulder. "As good Christians we had to become criminal,"[6] said Gertrud Staewen from the Berlin discussion group around Karl Barth. She was part of a resistance group which helped Berlin Jews to disappear — with forged passes and stolen food coupons. Dietrich Bonhoeffer was a regular resource person and contact with the Confessing Church.

At the end of 1942 Dietrich wrote a kind of reckoning for himself and his fellow conspirators in the Abwehr: "We have been silent witnesses of evil deeds; we have been drenched by many storms; we have learned the arts of equivocation and pretense; experience has made us suspicious of others and kept us from being truthful and open; intolerable conflicts have

---

6. From a television interview with Gertrud Staewen.

worn us down and even made us cynical. Are we still of any use?"[7]

Hardly anyone had posed as consistently as Bonhoeffer the question of incurring guilt in borderline political situations and had then reflected on it. He did so on behalf of many Christians in the resistance who had been abandoned by their church. But he was also to be the only German Protestant theologian who would later play a role in the ecumenical movement, in the liberation churches and movements of South Africa and Latin America. By contrast, given the way in which the Lutheran bishops supported the state during the Nazi period, Bishop Meiser was only being consistent when he ostentatiously stayed away from the memorial celebrations for Bonhoeffer at Flossenbürg concentration camp in 1953 because Bonhoeffer was a member of the political resistance and not a church martyr.

Those who wanted to know had long been aware that the state itself had a criminal character. In 1942, at a conference in the Berlin suburb of Wannsee, the "Final Solution" of the "Jewish question" was decided on, the murder of millions of European Jews. At the same time an order was given authorizing the German Wehrmacht to liquidate civil political opponents in the Soviet Union and declaring a field day on the Soviet civil population. At least eleven million people fell victim to the policy of occupation and extermination in the Soviet Union alone. Dietrich was informed of this — and dismayed, when he read in a letter from a former Finkenwalde student, "In districts where there are partisans, women and children who are suspected of supplying partisans with provisions have to be killed by shooting them in the back of the neck. These people have to be got rid of like that, because otherwise it is a

---

7. Bonhoeffer, *Letters and Papers from Prison*, 16.

question of German soldiers' lives. We have had to burn down villages in the last three weeks from military necessity. . . ."[8]

Dietrich had such episodes in mind when he wrote: "The great masquerade of evil has played havoc with all our ethical concepts. For evil to appear disguised as light, charity, historical necessity, or social justice is quite bewildering to anyone brought up on our traditional ethical concepts. . . ." And, "From the perplexingly large number of possible decisions, the way of *duty* seems to be the sure way out. Here, what is commanded is accepted as what is most certain, and the responsibility for it rests on the commander, not on the person commanded. But no one who confines himself to the limits of duty ever goes so far as to venture, on his sole responsibility, to act in the only way that makes it possible to score a direct hit on evil and defeat it. The man of duty will in the end have to do his duty by the devil too."[9]

To any member of the resistance who read this in 1942 it was clear who was meant here. For so far all attempts at an overthrow had come to grief on the attitude of the leading military, without which a *coup d'état* had no hope. They appealed to their duty to be loyal to the "Führer," although Dohnanyi's "poison cupboard" contained reason enough for abandoning this loyalty. Klaus Bonhoeffer, who served as a go-between with civil resistance groups, despised the senior military, who had a red stripe on their trousers but no civil courage: "What has a big nose, red legs, and both feet in the mud? A German general!"[10]

---

8. Bethge, *Bonhoeffer,* 608.
9. Bonhoeffer, *Letters and Papers from Prison,* 4.
10. Communication from Emmi Bonhoeffer in Bethge (eds.), *Letzte Briefe im Widerstand,* 44f.

That does not mean that there were no opponents of
Hitler in the army. From 1938 there was a whole series of new
plans for killing him and overthrowing the government. And
Dohnanyi was everywhere, as later were Klaus and Dietrich
Bonhoeffer. Dietrich's family gradually became one of the many
centers of resistance. Rüdiger Schleicher, Ursula Bonhoeffer's
husband, meanwhile joined them. There were often meetings
in the home of Karl and Paula Bonhoeffer, or with Rüdiger
and Ursula Schleicher nearby. For many conversations the telephone was covered with cushions. People made sure that none
of the servants was listening at the door. In the meantime it
had become clear to all the Bonhoeffers that now no one could
avoid social responsibility any longer.

On 12 March 1943 Eberhard Bethge drove Hans von
Dohnanyi in Karl Bonhoeffer's car to the railway station, the
Berlin Ostbahnhof. In Dohnanyi's briefcase was a special kind
of English explosive which he and Canaris were transporting
to Smolensk. The General Staff of the Central Army Group,
the senior officer of which was Henning von Tresckow, were
stationed there. Von Tresckow was one of the conspirators, and
was to smuggle the explosive into the plane in which Hitler
was flying back to Germany after a visit to the Central Army
group. However, Hitler landed unharmed in East Prussia: the
fuses of both time bombs had failed.

Hitler returned a week later. The booty of the Central
Army Group was put on display to celebrate "Heroes' Memorial
Day." Protocol provided for a half-hour visit by the Führer.
Major von Gersdorff was to accompany him. He had two
bombs in his briefcase. But Hitler ended the visit after only
ten minutes. In Berlin the conspirators waited in vain for the
codeword to start the uprising.

Eberhard Bethge, who meanwhile had been let into the

secret, recalls: "On that Sunday morning the family with all the grandchildren was practicing in the Schleichers' house the birthday cantata for the seventy-fifth birthday of Bonhoeffer's father. Dietrich Bonhoeffer was at the piano, Klaus was playing the cello, Rüdiger Schleicher the violin, and Hans Dohnanyi was in the choir. At the front door, Dohnanyi's car was ready to leave. . . ."[11] Dohnanyi kept looking at the clock, waiting for the decisive telephone call. His wife Christine, with whom he had discussed everything, shared his disquiet. She whispered to her sister Ursula Schleicher, "It must go off at any moment." But the call that was so urgently expected did not come. Instead, two weeks later the Gestapo arrived. With this, a year of detailed conspiratorial work came to nothing. The role that Dietrich played in it could only be reconstructed gradually, after the end of the Third Reich. It was part of being a conspirator that one should know only the barest essentials.

Between 1940 and 1943 Dietrich travelled to Switzerland on a number of occasions. The base of the provisional World Council of Churches was in Geneva. The General Secretary Visser 't Hooft was the intermediary for conversations between the German resistance movement and representatives of the churches in the West. From the beginning, Dietrich represented the radical group in the resistance, which called for the complete abolition of the Hitler régime. The hope was that if this were to happen, the allied forces would give the new German government a military respite and political support. The aim was the speediest possible cease-fire and a rapid peace treaty.

However, that was not the only version current in these conversations. The ideas of what would come after Hitler were

---

11. Bethge, *Bonhoeffer*, 685.

Above left: *Karl Barth*. Above right: *Klaus Bonhoeffer*.
Below left: *Hans von Dohnanyi*. Below right: *Rüdiger Schleicher*.

as varied as the German resistance movement itself. In some resistance groups people still wanted to win; in others to rescue what could be rescued. Some thought in terms of a democratic post-war Germany, others of a monarchical régime. Many wanted peace with the West, so as still to be able to win the war in the East despite the defeat at Stalingrad. That is one reason why the English involved in the discussion with whom Dietrich had connections were reserved about the requests and the communications which he brought.

The only one who trusted him was his friend from his London days, Bishop Bell of Chichester. Dietrich broke off a journey to Switzerland in 1942 to meet him in Stockholm. To their surprise, the two friends met on 31 May in the guest room of the Bishop of Sigtuna. Dietrich had just come off a stormy flight, with a courier's pass and a list of names in his luggage: possible members of the government after the overthrow. It was meant to indicate that there was the "other Germany." Bell promised to inform the English government and hoped for their agreement. However, on 23 July he sent a telegram to Visser 't Hooft in Geneva, "Interest undoubted, but deeply regret no reply possible." As long as there was no visible sign of German resistance, people saw no reason to distinguish between Nazis and Germans.

Two other missions which Bonhoeffer carried out as an Abwehr agent were more a matter of "damage limitation." At the beginning of April 1942 two emissaries of the Abwehr traveled to Norway. A church struggle had flared up there against the Norwegian Nazi Prime Minister Quisling. All the pastors and bishops had resigned. The instigator of the pastors' strike, Bishop Eivind Berggrav, had been arrested. However, on 15 April he was released on Bormann's instructions. The emissaries had warned that the church struggle would unnecessarily endanger the security of the German occupation forces. These emissaries were Dietrich Bonhoeffer and Helmut James Graf von Moltke. Both encouraged the Norwegians in their resistance.

Finally there was U7, "Operation 7," in which a group of German Jews (originally there were to have been seven) were to be smuggled into Switzerland disguised as Abwehr agents. This was to have far-reaching consequences. Operation 7 was successful, but for the resistance group in the Abwehr it was the beginning of the end. In the autumn of 1942 a conspirator in the Munich office of the Abwehr was interrogated over currency irregularities. That gave the Abwehr's rivals, the Reich Security Head Office — which in contrast to the Abwehr was directly under the Nazis — the opportunity to put the Munich Abwehr department under close scrutiny. They came upon traces of Operation 7 and the names of Dietrich Bonhoeffer and Hans von Dohnanyi. They still had no precise information, but from then on both Hans and Dietrich expected to be arrested. No one knew how long fellow conspirators could hold out under interrogation.

Hans and Dietrich attempted to cover their tracks and lay false trails. False letters and diary entries were written and placed carefully for the house search which threatened. But at the same time the preparations for the overthrow went on.

It is hard to imagine how those involved felt in such circumstances. What is reported of Dietrich at this time indicates that with the proximity of danger and death the intensity and joy in his life tended rather to increase. "There remains for us only the very narrow way, often extremely difficult to find, of living every day as if it were our last, and yet living in faith and responsibility as though there were to be a great future. . . . It may be that the day of judgment will dawn tomorrow; in that case, we shall gladly stop working for a better future. But not before,"[12] he wrote at Christmas 1942.

During this period Dietrich made his will. That was one thing. And he fell in love. That was the other. But even more was happening. "Saint" Dietrich Bonhoeffer, the Finkenwalde "abbot without mitre and crozier,"[13] was gradually becoming a thoroughly normal man.

In the summer of 1942 he wrote to Eberhard Bethge: "My activities, which have lately been very much in the worldly sector, give me plenty to think about. I am surprised that I live, and can go on living, for days without the Bible. . . . When I open the Bible again, it is ever so new and cheering. . . . I know that I only need to open my own books to hear what there is to be said against all this. . . . But I feel how my resistance to everything 'religious' is growing. . . . I am not religious by nature. But I always have to be thinking of God and of Christ, and I set great store by genuineness, life, freedom and compassion. Only I find the religious trappings so uncomfortable. Do you understand? These ideas and insights are not new at all, but as I think I shall now be able to see my way through them, I am letting things take their course. . . ."[14]

Something shifted imperceptibly in Dietrich's feelings about life. To live beyond the bounds of security no longer meant cutting oneself off from life and love. And at the very moment when Dietrich's inner distancing began to vanish, he met a woman who had enough energy to disconcert the unapproachable bachelor.

---

12. Bonhoeffer, *Letters and Papers from Prison*, 15.

13. Wilhelm Rott, in Zimmermann (ed.), *I Knew Dietrich Bonhoeffer*, 131.

14. Letter of 25 June 1942, in Bethge, *Bonhoeffer*, 626.

Maria von Wedemeyer was eighteen, Dietrich was thirty-six. She had known him for quite a long while, since his time in Finkenwalde. However, at that time Dietrich had been the pastor, and Maria the little sister of one of his confirmation candidates — and in the eyes of the strict Pastor Bonhoeffer a very self-willed child. Maria's grandmother, Ruth von Kleist-Retzow, had supported the Finkenwalde students as much as she could. Dietrich had entertained friends on her estate in Klein-Krössin, and had given lectures and had holidays there. Even in the years of the conspiracy he withdrew to work and rest on the estate in Pomerania. The elderly Ruth von Kleist-Retzow admired Dietrich and supported him in his radical views and uncompromising stand to such a degree that it almost proved too much for her relations. Anyway, Maria's mother was not particularly enthusiastic when in summer 1942, under the eyes of the radical old lady, a relationship developed between her daughter and a man twice her age, who at this time was anything but a "good match." She insisted on a year's separation, but the couple could not take it. Letters went to and fro. They became engaged — by correspondence. In the spring, Maria, with the help of her brother and her brother-in-law Klaus von Bismarck, tried to persuade her mother to change her mind. She did not want to wait any longer for a reunion with Dietrich. The two men expressed their readiness for a conversation, but they came with bad news — that of Dietrich's arrest.[15]

---

15. Communication to me by Ruth-Alice von Bismarck née von Wedemeyer, 26 April 1990.

Learning to Believe in the
This-Worldliness of Life

---------------------------- 1943–1944 ----------------------------

O N 5 APRIL 1943, DIETRICH TELEPHONED HIS PARENTS'
home from the Dohnanyis'. However, an unknown male
voice answered the telephone. So he knew that something was
up; he checked to see that his desk was "clean" and invited
himself to the Schleichers' nearby for a good lunch. There he
waited with Eberhard Bethge for the Gestapo. Around four
o'clock he was asked over; Judge Advocate Roeder and Gestapo
Commissioner Sonderegger were waiting for him. After a brief
questioning Dietrich was arrested and taken to Tegel, the Wehrmacht interrogation prison.

"For the first night I was locked up in an admission cell.
The blankets on the camp bed had such a foul smell that in
spite of the cold it was impossible to use them. The next
morning a piece of bread was thrown into my cell; I had to
pick it up from the floor. . . . The sound of the prison staff's
vile abuse of the prisoners who were held for investigation
penetrated into my cell for the first time; since then I have
heard it every day from morning to night. . . . The tone is set

by those warders who behave in the most evil and brutal way towards the prisoners."[1]

The next day Dietrich was put in a cell of his own. For twelve days no one spoke a word to him. He was not allowed to write or receive any letters. No one told him the reason for his imprisonment or how long it would last. In the night he was haunted by the noises from the neighboring cells, the cries of those condemned to death, who were fettered day and night.

When the ban on contact was lifted on 14 April, Dietrich wrote a letter to his parents which was a brilliant piece of self-control and Bonhoefferian discipline over the senses: "Dear parents, I do want you to be quite sure that I'm all right. . . . Strangely enough, the discomforts that one generally associates with prison life, the physical hardships, hardly bother me at all."[2]

What it was really like in prison can be seen in the words written on the other side of the note-pad on which the contents of food parcels had to be listed — in the first weeks the only writing material which Dietrich had. "Separation from people, from work, from the past, from the future, from marriage, from God, impatience, longing, boredom, sick — profoundly alone, suicide, not because of consciousness of guilt but because basically I am already dead. Line. Total. Overcoming in prayer."[3]

Two things preoccupied Dietrich most: the feeling of helplessness, the unusual experience that he was no longer master of his own time — and the enforced loneliness precisely at the point at which he had broken out of his inner reserve. Those in charge of the interrogation by the Gestapo were good

---

1. Bonhoeffer, *Letters and Papers from Prison*, 248.
2. Ibid., 21.
3. Bethge and Gremmels (eds.), *Dietrich Bonhoeffer. A Life in Pictures*, 191.

psychologists. They quickly discovered the weak points of their victims. Weeks of uncertainty and isolation would make the prisoners pliable. And when the interrogations began they threatened torture and reprisals against Dietrich's parents and fiancée.

Dietrich needed all his strength to keep his nerve and his will to live. Later he would tell fellow prisoners openly that in certain situations he regarded suicide as understandable and forgivable — to protect others and not to betray fellow conspirators. He frankly conceded that he feared torture. He was far too fond of life not to be afraid of torture and of not being able to stand up to it.

Roeder, who led the interrogation, was notorious for his methods: at the beginning of 1943 he had wiped out the Red Chapel resistance group. Seventy-five death sentences were handed out: the victims included Arvid Harnack, a nephew of Dietrich's old teacher Adolf von Harnack. A number of members of the group died during the hearings as a result of maltreatment, or were forced to commit suicide.

Dietrich knew too much to have any illusions. Readiness for suicide was the last piece of freedom left him — and so it was almost a support for the impending hearings. And it was urgently necessary. For the important thing was not just to avoid mentioning names but also not to endanger the ongoing planning for the overthrow. The Gestapo and the Reich Security Head Office still had no detailed knowledge. However, they suspected that Canaris's office had got out of control. With Bonhoeffer and Dohnanyi they hoped that they had found a thread by which they could unravel the resistance group in the Abwehr. However, they did not get any further. The pair managed to tangle the threads. They had prepared for the "emergency" well; and even now, in prison, the arrangement continued, in secret channels and by conspiratorial methods.

When the ban on contact was lifted, Dietrich had books sent to him, partly to read, and partly as a means of sending news. If a book came back in which Dietrich had underlined his name it meant that it contained a message. Every two pages, beginning from the back, a letter had been lightly marked with pencil. The news, mostly information from the interrogations, was deciphered by the family and passed on by similar secret channels to Dohnanyi, who was in the prison for more senior officials, and also to those fellow conspirators who were still free. In this way Dietrich and Hans managed not to be played off against each other. Roeder gnashed his teeth over Dohnanyi, the experienced lawyer, and even Dietrich was able to disguise his role. He played the innocent, politically inexperienced pastor who had always only worked for the best. No matter how much Roeder and Sonderegger of the Gestapo prodded, there was not enough for a charge of treason and high treason. There were not even enough hints to justify the usual methods of torture, at any rate with these accused, who were either related to influential scientists and soldiers or on friendly terms with them.

Dietrich had an adequate explanation for everything: for his exemption, for his conversations abroad, for Operation 7. In Protestantism, hitherto there had been no ethical reflections on the need to lie and disguise oneself. Now Dietrich began them. "What is meant by telling the truth?" was smuggled out of his cell as a fragment and hidden in the loft at the Bonhoeffers'.

"Our speech must be truthful, not in principle but concretely. A truthfulness which is not concrete is not truthful before God. 'Telling the truth,' therefore, is not solely a matter of moral character; it is also a matter of correct appreciation of real situations and of serious reflection upon them. The more complex the actual situations of a man's life, the more responsible and difficult will be his task of 'telling the truth.'"4

When Dietrich wrote these lines in the summer of 1943 he had the first crisis of prison and the decisive interrogations already behind him. He was allowed to read and write, to send and receive a letter every ten days, and to have an hour's visit every month. Above all he had found ways of smuggling texts and letters from the cell past the censor. The friendly prisoner, who in the meantime had again become quite sovereign, had won over some of his guards. They enjoyed talking with him and did him some favors. In this way the letters to Eberhard Bethge all got out uncensored.

There is a selection of them in *Letters and Papers from Prison*. They begin on 18 November 1943 and contain breathtaking beginnings of a new theology, reflections on a "religionless Christianity" in a "world come of age." In them Dietrich found his real theme, his real language, his identity. But before that, he went through a personal crisis which led him deep into a controversy with the past and at the same time made possible a breakthrough to new beginnings.

The occasion for this crisis seems first of all to have been external. After the end of the interrogation phase and the first relaxations, prison became a nerve-racking test of patience. Influential friends and adverse circumstances delayed the date of the trial from which Dietrich hoped for freedom. He was constantly disappointed. Those who were pulling strings in the background on his behalf had good reasons for letting the

---

4. Bonhoeffer, *Ethics*, 386f.

proceedings run into the sand until the overthrow. On the one hand they feared that something else might still come to light which had been successfully concealed so far. On the other hand, they reckoned that Hans and Dietrich might not be freed, but "released" into a concentration camp — and compared with that, the Wehrmacht prison was an almost safer place.

Dietrich more or less realized this, but found it difficult to come to terms with. So far, his life had shaped itself. Now other people were controlling him and he had to wait for things to happen. He often had the feeling that life was passing him by. His prison existence consisted in waiting — waiting until he could again take part in "real life."

But things got even worse. Dietrich felt that he was in danger of inwardly losing the ground under his feet. Certainly he was anything but a "settled person" and he had never regretted the step beyond the limits of middle-class security. However, he would not have been able to sustain this life-style without firm roots in the family, in friends, in the "communion of saints." What had been home for him now came into his life only for moments — through a letter, a visit — and at every parting the world from which he came and to which he belonged seemed to shatter a bit more.

In this crisis, in the "emptiness of time," Dietrich attempted to work on the past creatively. For a while he returned to the world of his childhood. He began to write a play and a novel about a middle-class family — his own. He broke off both attempts when he saw that little more than trivia were coming out of them.

He himself would certainly never have published these Tegel fragments. They probably had more of a therapeutic function. "This dialogue with the past, the attempt to hold on to it and recover it, and above all, the fear of losing it, is the almost daily accompaniment of my life here. . . ."[5]

For a while this crisis made Dietrich regress and take refuge in a sound, past world. That, at any rate, is the interpretation of the American historian Ruth Zerner. Only when he had been able to work through this crisis creatively could he overcome it and formulate a new approach to life and thought.

First of all, however, he returned almost uncritically to the ordered world of the middle-class: "In my reading I am now living entirely in the nineteenth century. During these months I've read Gotthelf, Stifter, Immermann, Fontane, and Keller with new admiration."[6] Copying their style, he painted the picture of a past world in which the order which shaped him still prevailed. Dietrich, who had already moved out of himself so far, displayed a conservatism which no longer really fitted him.

The young woman, who in the novel was to have features of Maria, was "not one of those daughters of our time who wasted their days at cocktail parties, tea dances, and the worship of film stars. She wasn't one of those emancipated half-men. . . . She was a born mother who had experienced the joy of a good family life from her childhood and now carried it within her as a possession she could never lose." And Christoph, who in the fragment of the play stands for Dietrich, reports that in a debate on civic freedom he had said, "One should never make freedom a slogan for the masses, because from that would arise the worst kind of slavery. Freedom is only for the very few, noble, select people. . . . There must be upper and lower posi-

5. Letter of 5 June 1944, in Bonhoeffer, *Letters and Papers from Prison*, 319.

6. Ibid., 78.

tions among men. . . . there are men, noble by nature, who are destined to rule and be free, and there are people who are by nature rabble, and they must serve."[7]

Such remarks go against everything that Dietrich developed later in his "theology of the prison letters." In them the gospel has a clear tendency "from above downwards," and compels solidarity with the underdogs and the option for the sufferers. The American theologian T. J. Day was struck by the "contradiction between the gospel which Dietrich wanted to keep track of and the authoritarian structures in which he attempted to live. In the end the gospel had to break out of this framework."[8]

Imprisoned with himself and his history, Dietrich arrived at a critical assimilation and finally a "conversion," a re-orientation in his situation. Reading the gospel, the "good news" of liberation for solidarity, once again led him anew and finally to go beyond the bounds of the background of his class. The man of law and order became a liberation theologian. And the liberation also changed Dietrich himself.

But other people, too, helped Dietrich to see the world and himself in yet another way — simply by being different from what his traditional notions had led him to expect. Above all there was Maria, who did not at all correspond to the conservative ideal of womanhood that Dietrich had painted. After the war she was to study mathematics and later hold a leading position in a computer firm in the United States; at that time she did not dream of admiring the great theologian uncritically or allowing herself to be shaped by

---

7. Bonhoeffer, *Fiction from Prison*, 98, 21f.
8. T. J. Day, *The Meaning of Christian Community for Dietrich Bonhoeffer*, New York 1975, 630.

him. Her sister Ruth-Alice von Bismarck recalls, rather, an emancipated relationship between the two unequal partners. Of course Maria was in love with Dietrich and of course she stood by him; but she also stood, for example, by her beloved Rilke, whom Dietrich found "unhealthy." When she did not agree with Dietrich, she contradicted him. Evidently Dietrich liked that; he felt that she was his match in discussion. We might even suppose that she played a far greater part in bringing him back onto firm ground than is generally assumed.

In June 1943, Maria and Dietrich met again — in the presence of Judge Advocate Roeder. Now Maria was given permission to visit and write regularly. And gradually the picture which Dietrich had made for himself of her became a real person. What irritated and fascinated him about her was not just her independence. Unlike him, she did not restrain her feelings. She told him that he must not keep holding back his feelings from her. "In *your* family people have learned to show feelings," Dietrich is said to have replied.[9]

In his relationship with Maria, Dietrich's emotions were increasingly set free. But that did not make his situation any simpler. Above all when it proved that no speedy end to his imprisonment was in sight, the tension became almost intolerable for the two of them. They had to live in the awareness that their relationship might remain unfulfilled. They had constantly to meet each other and part at the same time.

In May 1944, after a visit from Maria, Dietrich wrote a poem for the first time. In it there is a remarkable mixture of his longing for Maria and his grief over a past life.

---

9. Communication of Ruth-Alice von Bismarck, 26 April 1990.

O happiness beloved, and pain beloved in heaviness,
you went from me.
What shall I call you? Anguish, life, blessedness,
part of myself, my heart — the past?
The door was slammed;
I hear your steps depart and slowly die away.
What now remains for me — torment, delight, desire?
This only do I know: that with you, all has gone.
But do you feel how I now grasp at you . . .
that it must hurt you . . .
simply to be sure that you are near me,
a life in earthly form, complete?[10]

The poem is one long outburst of feeling. Dietrich first sent it to Eberhard Bethge, asking him whether he should also give it to Maria. But probably behind this was also the question whether he might concede his feelings, his longing, his grief to himself.

That he did so without despairing of his situation was probably also the result of his capacity to express his feelings in letters and above all in poems which he now composed. The Bonhoeffer principle of not letting go of oneself once again proved productive. But it was the emotion opened up in his relationship with Maria which made it possible for him to free himself from stereotyped pictures of her and himself, to come alive and become himself.

The correspondence between Maria and Dietrich has not been published. Maria has left it in her will to a theological faculty in the USA.

We learn from the letters to Eberhard Bethge that his

---

10. Bonhoeffer, *Letters and Papers from Prison*, 320.

Above left: *Maria von Wedemeyer.* Above right: *The cell at Tegel prison.*
Below: *In the yard at Tegel prison, together with captured officers of the
Italian air force, early summer 1944.*

fellow prisoners, his companions in suffering, also made Dietrich think again. But that became possible only when Dietrich no longer felt his life in prison to be a separation from "real" life. Now he would gradually also accept the Tegel prison as his world, and make new and surprising discoveries in it.

First of all, the people whom he met there took on individual features and sharper contours. That was also because conditions in prison changed. In the meantime the friendly pastor and prominent prisoner had become more forthcoming. He had enough to read and eat, and he could move relatively freely; prisoners and guards enjoyed talking to him. After the air raids which also caused deaths and casualties in Tegel prison, he was called on to provide first aid. He got to know people from a very wide variety of social backgrounds. It impressed him that people who were shaped neither by Christian faith nor by middle-class education could be wise companions in the struggle, thoughtful and ready to help — while in his own camp, in the church and the middle class, he had to fight against opportunism and accommodation. Dietrich's views of the élite and the rabble were turned upside down. Even those proletarian prisoners who remained alien to him were part of the community to which he now belonged. Dietrich no longer kept his distance; in the emergency community of Tegel he gave and experienced solidarity.

Gospel and life became identical: "There remains an experience of incomparable value, that we have learned to see the great events of world history for once from below, from the perspective of those who are excluded, suspected, maltreated, powerless, oppressed, and scorned, in short the sufferers."[11] Once again Dietrich asked what it meant to be a disciple of Jesus.

---

11. *Gesammelte Schriften* II, 441.

His answer reflected both the reading of the gospel and his own practice: "Jesus asked in Gethsemane, 'Could you not watch with me one hour?' That is a reversal of what the religious man expects from God. . . . It is not the religious act that makes the Christian, but participation in the sufferings of God in the secular life. . . . Jesus calls men, not to a new religion, but to life."[12]

That brought Dietrich to his great theme: "We are entering into a completely religionless time. People simply cannot be religious any longer, as they once were. . . . Where is there still room for God?" The answer leads in a radical way to life in this world. "God is the beyond in the midst of our life. The God who is with us is the God who forsakes us."[13] Such statements are the consequence of *The Cost of Discipleship*. Jesus died without disciples. Without people who live and act, God remains invisible.

Dietrich kept stressing that God may not be brought in to solve problems which people must tackle themselves: "Religious people speak of God when human knowledge (perhaps simply because they are too lazy to think) has come to an end or where human resources fail — in fact it is always the *deus ex machina* that they bring on the scene . . . always exploiting human weakness or human boundaries. I should like to speak of God . . . not in weaknesses but in strength; and therefore not in death and guilt but in man's life and goodness. As to the boundaries, it seems to me better to be silent and leave the insoluble unsolved."[14]

That fits what he wrote to Eberhard Bethge after a heavy air raid: "As we were again lying on the floor last night, and

---

12. Bonhoeffer, *Letters and Papers from Prison*, 361f.
13. Ibid., 360.
14. Ibid., 281f.

someone exclaimed 'O God, O God' (he is normally a very flippant type), I couldn't bring myself to offer him any Christian encouragement of comfort; all I did was to look at my watch and say, 'It won't last more than ten minutes now.' There was nothing premeditated about it; it came quite automatically, and perhaps I thought that it was wrong to force religion down his throat just then."[15] And finally, "I certainly won't get out of here a religious person! On the contrary, my mistrust and anxiety about being religious have become greater than ever. I keep reflecting on how the Israelites *never* uttered the name of God, and I keep understanding it better."[16]

Dietrich kept on hearing too clearly the phrases with which his church had praised the Führer, people, and fatherland. Moreover, the attempt in this historical catastrophe to withdraw into preaching guilt and redemption seemed to him to be no less incredible: "What reconciliation and redemption are, rebirth and the Holy Spirit, love of one's enemy, cross and resurrection, the meaning of life in Christ and discipleship of Christ, is all so difficult and so remote that we hardly dare to speak of it. . . . That is our own guilt. Our church, which over these years has fought only for its self-preservation as though that were an end in itself, is incapable of being the vehicle of the reconciling and redeeming word for human beings and the world. So the former words must become powerless and fall silent, and our being Christians today must consist of two things: in praying and doing what is right among men."[17]

For Dietrich, praying and doing what was right were two sides of the same coin: he who wanted to live and act "as if

---

15. Ibid., 199.
16. Quoted in Gremmels and Pfeifer, *Theologie und Biographie*, 117.
17. Ibid., 126.

there were no God" — at any rate, not the God who relieved him of acting! — at the same time turned to the God from whom all hope springs and in whom all life is lifted up. To be bound to an authority in which love, justice, and reconciliation exist once for all, beyond human control, remained for Dietrich the last abiding stay. "O God, early in the morning I cry to you. Help me to pray and to concentrate my thoughts on you; I cannot do this alone."[18]

He described what he himself had to do and what he had to leave to God in "Stations on the Road to Freedom":

Action

Daring to do what is right, not what fancy may tell you,
valiantly grasping occasions, not cravenly doubting —
freedom comes only through deeds, not through
    thoughts taking wing.

Suffering

A change has come indeed. Your hands, so strong
    and active,
are bound; in helplessness now you see your action
is ended; . . .
Only for one blissful moment could you draw near
    to touch freedom;
then, that it might be perfected in glory, you gave it
    to God.[19]

---

18. Bonhoeffer, *Letters and Papers from Prison*, 139.
19. Ibid., 370f.

In this limitation of what one can do oneself, Dietrich's attempt to become something like a saint also came to an end: "One must completely abandon any attempt to make something of oneself, whether it be a saint, or a converted sinner, or a churchman. In so doing we throw ourselves completely into the arms of God, taking seriously, not our own sufferings, but those of God in the world — watching with Christ in Gethsemane. That, I think, is faith."[20]

That was also Dietrich's personal liberation from the pressure to be something special. Increasingly there appears in the letters from Tegel someone who like anyone else longs to be free, to love his wife, have children, and live in peace. One evening in May 1944 he wrote to Eberhard: "I find these long, warm evenings, which I'm now living through here for the second time, rather trying. . . . When you've deliberately suppressed every desire for so long, it may have one of two bad results: either it burns you up inside, or it all gets so bottled up that one day there is a terrific explosion. It is, of course, conceivable that one may become completely selfless, and I know better than anyone else that that hasn't happened to me."[21]

Those are quite frank remarks for the detached Dietrich. In fact somewhere a penny has finally dropped. The last photograph of Dietrich comes from this summer and shows someone who has accepted the quite normal human side in himself. Full of hope and impatience, he is waiting for the overthrow which he has helped to prepare for.

On 20 July 1944 the news flash even reached the prison cells in Tegel: an attempt had been made on the life of the

---

20. Ibid., 369f.
21. Ibid., 312.

Führer. However, by nightfall all hopes had been dashed. Hitler had survived the attack; Colonel Stauffenberg, who had placed the bomb, had been shot along with his closest collaborators, and the first wave of arrests was already under way.

On 21 July 1944 the Evangelical Church declared: "While our bold and courageous armies have been engaged in heavy fighting to protect the homeland and win the final victory, a handful of despicable officers driven on by ambition have dared the most dreadful crime and attempted to kill the Führer. The Führer was saved, and so our people has been spared unspeakable disaster. We are grateful to God with all our hearts. . . ."[22]

The same day Dietrich wrote Eberhard a letter which is almost like a testament. He reckoned that sooner or later he would be caught up in the downfall of the opposition and gave an account of his own way.

"During the last year or so I've come to know and understand more and more the profound this-worldliness of Christianity. The Christian is not a *homo religiosus* but simply a man, as Jesus was a man. . . . I thought that I could acquire faith by trying to live a holy life, or something like that. . . . I discovered later, and I'm still discovering right up to this moment, that it is only by living completely in this world that one learns to have faith."[23]

---

22. Bethge and Gremmels (eds.), *Dietrich Bonhoeffer. A Life in Pictures,* 221.

23. Bonhoeffer, *Letters and Papers from Prison,* 369.

The End
Is the Beginning

---------------- 1944–1945 ----------------

O N 5 OCTOBER 1944 THE GESTAPO COMMISSAR WALTER
Huppenkothen went into the sick bay of Sachsenhausen
concentration camp where Hans von Dohnanyi was held with
serious diphtheria, and paralyzed in both legs. He threw a
document on the bed and said, "There! At last we've got the
evidence against you we've been looking for for two years."
Dohnanyi had to get a grip of himself before answering in an
apparently disinterested way, "Oh, have you? Where did you
find it?"[1]

In a branch of the Abwehr in Zossen, at the end of
September secret papers had been found in a safe, including
the memorandum which Dohnanyi had produced as early as
1939 to persuade the German generals to attempt a *coup d'état*.
The "Zossen documents" gave an amazing view of the extent
and duration of the conspiracy. They set off a new wave of
arrests. A number of hasty trials were arranged, and those under
arrest were subjected to renewed and "intensified" interroga-

---

1. Notes made by Christine von Dohnanyi, in Bethge, *Bonhoeffer*, 714.

172

tion. Hans wrote to his wife in a note which had been smuggled out with a bundle of laundry: "They have everything, absolutely everything, against me, and in my own hand."[2] He asked her to smuggle dysentery bacteria into prison. His only chance of survival lay in remaining unfit to stand trial. In the meantime it had become clear to everyone that the end was in sight for the war and thus for Nazi rule. For those imprisoned and condemned, liberation by the allied force was the only hope which remained.

Dietrich's situation also deteriorated at a stroke with the discovery of the Zossen documents. For now it became clear what role he had in fact played. Moreover all those who could have protected him had themselves been arrested. The Abwehr had been dissolved, Canaris had been arrested, and Paul von Hase, City commandant of Berlin and Dietrich's uncle, had already been executed. But help came once again, this time from quite a different side. One of the Tegel guards, Corporal Knobloch, offered to disappear with Dietrich. Knobloch was a worker from north Berlin, an opponent of Hitler, and for months the secret courier between Dietrich and the outside world. Many illegals had been hidden in the summer houses among the allotments of the working-class districts of Berlin; why not now a pastor from Grunewald?

The family gave Knobloch a parcel with overalls for Dietrich, money, and food coupons. The escape attempt was to start at the beginning of October. But on 1 October Klaus Bonhoeffer was arrested. On 2 October Knobloch informed the family that Dietrich had abandoned the plan to escape so as not to endanger his brother and the rest of the family.

---

2. Bethge, in Bethge (ed.), *Letzte Briefe im Widerstand,* 85.

Dietrich Bonhoeffer in the yard at Tegel prison, summer 1944

No one quite knows what went through Dietrich's mind at this time. As in New York, the decision which he made was probably connected with his inability to leave the "battle front" and the company of his fellow sufferers. And so that there can be life where one loses it.

On 4 October Rüdiger Schleicher was arrested, and some time later also Eberhard Bethge, who in the meantime had married the Schleichers' oldest daughter. He was the only one of those from the family circle who were arrested to survive the end of the Nazi régime.

On 8 October Dietrich was removed from Tegel and transferred to the notorious basement of the Reich Security Head Office in Prinz-Albrecht-Strasse. A fellow prisoner, the Italian officer Gaetano Latmiral, who later became a professor, reported that Dietrich said good-bye to his friend as though nothing had happened. But his eyes had been unnaturally bright. Dietrich became a saint at the very moment when he did not want to.

There was no more news of Dietrich from Prinz-Albrecht-Strasse. No one was allowed to talk to him. Only two letters reached his parents; one contained a poem which Dietrich had written at the end of the year for his mother and Maria:

With every power for good to stay and guide me,
comforted and inspired beyond all fear,
I'll live these days with you in thought beside me,
and pass, with you, into the coming year.

The old year still torments our hearts, unhastening,
the long days of our sorrow still endure,
Father, grant to the souls thou hast been chastening
that thou hast promised, the healing and the cure.

Should it be ours to drain the cup of grieving
even to the dregs of pain, at thy command,
we will not falter, thankfully receiving
all that is given by thy loving hand.

But should it be thy will once more to release us
to life's enjoyment and its good sunshine,
that which we've learned from sorrow shall increase us,
and all our life be dedicate as thine.

Today, let candles shed their radiant greeting;
lo, on our darkness are they not thy light,
leading us, haply, to our longed-for meeting? —
Thou canst illumine even our darkest night.

When now the silence deepens for our hearkening,
grant we may hear thy children's voices raise
from all the unseen world around us darkening
their universal paean, in thy praise.

While all the powers of good aid and attend us,
boldly we'll face the future, come what may.
At even and at morn God will befriend us,
and oh, most surely on each new born day.[3]

The last verse is nowadays a popular motto on calendars and postcards from Christian publishers, usually illustrated with a sunset or candlelight. This false idyll does not do justice to the drama which is expressed in the poem: that someone has come to the point at which he can affirm both life and death.

---

3. Bonhoeffer, *Letters and Papers from Prison*, 400.

Dietrich's existence moved between these two possibilities in the last months of his life in an almost dramatic way. Probably only those can withstand the searing test of having to prepare at the same time for both life and death who can die because they have really learned to live, and who can live because they have come to terms with their death.

At the beginning of the war Dietrich had written that there was a death from outside and a death from within, which belongs to us: "We may pray that death from without does not come to us till we have been made ready for it through this inherent death; then our death is really only the gateway to the perfect love of God."[4]

In the meantime the People's Court under the presidency of the notorious Roland Freisler had been wreaking a regular massacre among the middle-class opposition. Almost five thousand people fell victim to this last wave of terror. On 2 February 1945 Klaus Bonhoeffer and Rüdiger Schleicher were also condemned to death.

On 3 February a severe bombing attack reduced part of the justice building and the Reich Security Head Office to rubble and ashes.

Dietrich's parents were also caught in the air raid warning, trying to bring their son a parcel to the prison for his thirty-ninth birthday. His father wrote a typical Bonhoeffer letter: "Dear Dietrich, Because of the attack our birthday letter didn't get into your hands. We sat in Anhalt station in the S-Bahn during the attack; it wasn't very attractive. Nothing happened, except that afterwards we looked like chimney sweeps. Afterwards, however, when we tried to visit you, we were very disturbed because we weren't allowed in because of the unex-

---

4. Bethge, *Bonhoeffer*, 743.

ploded bombs. The next day we heard that nothing had happened to the prisoners. We hope that that is true."[5]

The letter and the parcel were the last news that Dietrich received from his family. On the afternoon of the same day he was taken off to an unknown destination. Only on the next day when a parcel was allowed, 14 February, did Maria and his parents learn that he was no longer in Berlin. No one could or would say where he had been taken.

In the meantime Dietrich and other members of the Abwehr resistance had been imprisoned in the bunker of Buchenwald concentration camp. His fellow prisoners also included some prominent foreigners like the English airman Payne Best and Molotov's nephew Kokorin from Moscow. Dietrich became friends with both of them in the next few weeks. Best recalled: "Bonhoeffer was all humility and sweetness; he always seemed to diffuse an atmosphere of happiness, of joy in every smallest event in life, and of deep gratitude for the mere fact that he was alive."[6]

Dietrich was introduced to Russian by Kokorin and Kokorin was introduced to the Bible by Dietrich. No one knew precisely what was in store for them. But since the fronts and the communication systems were collapsing all around, there was less and less expectation that there would be a trial in the general downfall of the Third Reich.

At the beginning of April shots could already be heard in Buchenwald from the approaching American forces. So on 3 April the VIP prisoners and the hard cases were transported away. They went south in a sluggish wood-burning truck. A destination was mentioned which struck terror among the

---

5. Bonhoeffer, *Letters and Papers from Prison,* 403.
6. Bethge, *Bonhoeffer,* 823.

occupants: Flossenbürg concentration camp was known to be an extermination camp.

But the transport went past Flossenbürg. There was great relief, until the journey was again interrupted and three prisoners were taken out. Dietrich was not among them. With the others he ended up in Regensburg and finally in a school in Schönberg, twenty-five miles north of Passau. Here there were proper beds and a sack of potatoes. Payne Best passed his razor around. They sat by the window and sunned themselves. The danger seemed to be over.

On Sunday 8 April Dietrich was asked to hold a service; everyone wanted it, even Kokorin the atheist. Dietrich spoke on the reading for the day: "Blessed be the God and Father of our Lord Jesus Christ. By his great mercy we have been born anew to a living hope. . . ." He spoke of the hopes and plans which each would take with him from prison into freedom. When the service was ended, he was summoned: "Prisoner Bonhoeffer, get ready and come with us."

On 5 April 1945, in the noon discussion with Hitler, it was decided to liquidate the Abwehr resistance group with speedy trials. The next day Hans von Dohnanyi in Sachsenhausen was carried off on a stretcher to trial, and three days later to execution.

On 8 April the transport with Dietrich Bonhoeffer, who had almost escaped, arrived in Flossenbürg. The SS Judge Thorbeck condemned the Abwehr members of the resistance, including Canaris, Oster, and Bonhoeffer, to death for treason and high treason.

There is no direct evidence of Dietrich from these last hours. The last traces that he left in Schönberg are a book with his name and address in it and a message for Payne Best to take to his English friend George Bell. The camp doctor in

179

Flossenbürg reported that Dietrich had prayed before his execution and had been peaceful and composed.

Along with five other members of his resistance group, Dietrich Bonhoeffer was hanged in Flossenbürg concentration camp on the morning of 9 April 1945.

At the same time Maria was wandering through south Germany with a case full of warm clothing in the hope of finding Dietrich. Everywhere she was turned away, even in Flossenbürg. For months no one knew what had happened to Dietrich. His body had been burned along with thousands of others.

A month later the Third Reich came to an end. Germany capitulated unconditionally, and the allied troops stood uncomprehending before the mass graves of the concentration camps and extermination camps.

On 27 July 1945 a memorial service was broadcast by the BBC from Holy Trinity Church, Kingsway, in London. It was held by George Bell, Franz Hildebrandt, and Julius Rieger for Dietrich Bonhoeffer. Only now did his parents know that Dietrich was no longer alive.

In his sermon George Bell said that Dietrich had acted in the tradition of the prophets and the apostles. His confession of God had been bound up with the struggle against injustice. From this spirit grew the hope of a new life.

The last words which we have from Dietrich Bonhoeffer were intended for George Bell: "This is the end, for me the beginning of life. I believe in universal Christian brotherhood which rises above national interests and I believe that our victory is certain."[7]

---

7. Ibid., 830.

BIBLIOGRAPHY

Books by Dietrich Bonhoeffer

The Cost of Discipleship, SCM Press and Macmillan Publishing Company 1959

Life Together, SCM Press and Harper and Row 1954

Ethics, SCM Press and Macmillan Publishing Company 1955

Letters and Papers from Prison, edited by Eberhard Bethge, SCM Press and Macmillan Publishing Company, The Enlarged Edition 1971

Bonhoeffer for a New Generation, edited by Otto Dudzus, SCM Press 1985

Fiction from Prison, Fortress Press 1981

Jugend und Studium 1918–1927, Dietrich Bonhoeffer Werke, Vol. 9, edited by Hans Pfeifer in collaboration with Clifford Green and Carl-Jürgen Kaltenborn, Munich 1986

Gesammelte Schriften I–IV, ed. Eberhard Bethge, Munich 1958–61

A partial translation of these collected works has appeared in English in three volumes as follows:

Edwin Robertson (ed.), *No Rusty Swords,* Collins and Harper and Row ²1970

Edwin Robertson (ed.), *The Way to Freedom,* Collins and Harper and Row 1966

Edwin Robertson (ed.), *True Patriotism*, Collins and Harper and Row 1973

Literature about Bonhoeffer

Eberhard Bethge, *Dietrich Bonhoeffer. Theologian. Christian. Contemporary*, Collins and Harper and Row 1977

Eberhard Bethge, Renate Bethge, and Christian Gremmels (eds.), *Dietrich Bonhoeffer. A Life in Pictures*, SCM Press and Fortress Press 1986

Christian Gremmels and Hans Pfeifer, *Theologie und Biographie. Zum Beispiel Dietrich Bonhoeffer*, Munich 1983

Edwin Robertson, *The Shame and the Sacrifice. The Life and Teaching of Dietrich Bonhoeffer*, Hodder 1987

Sabine Leibholz-Bonhoeffer, *Vergangen — erlebt — überwunden. Schicksale der Familie Bonhoeffer*, Gütersloh 1985

Eberhard Bethge and Renate Bethge (eds.), *Letzte Briefe im Widerstand. Aus dem Kreis der Familie Bonhoeffer*, Munich [2]1988

Wolf-Dieter Zimmermann (ed.), *I Knew Dietrich Bonhoeffer*, Collins and Harper and Row 1966

Literature on contemporary history and church history

Irene Hübner (ed.), *Unser Widerstand. Deutsche Männer und Frauen berichten über ihren Kampf gegen die Nazis*, Frankfurt am Main 1982

Werner Koch, *Sollen wir K. wiederbeobachten? Ein Leben im Widerstand*, Stuttgart 1982

Karl Kupisch, *Kirchengeschichte V, 1815–1945*, Stuttgart 1975

Hans Prolingheuer, *Ausgetan aus dem Land der Lebendigen. Leidensgeschichten unter Kreuz und Hakenkreuz*, Neukirchen-Vluyn 1983

Hans Prolingheuer, *Kleine politische Kirchengeschichte. Fünfzig Jahre evangelischer Kirchenkampf von 1919 bis 1969*, Cologne 1984

Eberhard Röhm and Jörg Thierfelder (eds.), *Evangelische Kirche zwischen Kreuz und Hakenkreuz. Bilder und Texte einer Ausstellung*, Stuttgart [3]1983

Kurt Scharf, *Widerstehen und Versöhnen*, Stuttgart 1987